THE UNANIMITY RULE AND THE
LEAGUE OF NATIONS

AMS PRESS
NEW YORK

THE UNANIMITY RULE AND THE LEAGUE OF NATIONS

BY

CROMWELL A. RICHES, Ph. D.

Assistant Professor of Political Science, Goucher College
Instructor in Political Science, College for Teachers,
The Johns Hopkins University

BALTIMORE
THE JOHNS HOPKINS PRESS
1933

Reprinted from the edition of 1933: Baltimore

First AMS edition published in 1971

Manufactured in the United States of America

International Standard Book Number: 0-404-05330-0

Library of Congress Catalog Card Number: 70-174318

AMS PRESS INC.
NEW YORK, N.Y.   10003

To
Z. L. R.
and
M. E. R.

PREFACE

Much confusion exists concerning the extent to which the Council and the Assembly of the League of Nations adhere in practice to the rule of unanimity which had become accepted in the international " political " conferences of the nineteenth century. Article 5 of the Covenant lays down the general rule of unanimity for the Council and for the Assembly subject to such exceptions as are " expressly provided in this Covenant, or by the terms of the present treaty." However, publicists are by no means in agreement concerning the extent or the importance of the departures from the rule which are made in the actual practice of those two League organs. It is frequently asserted that unanimity, with trifling and unimportant exceptions, is always requisite in the Assembly, and in the Council as well. On the other hand, a few writers have stated that important decisions are now taken by majority vote, the voting becoming a reality rather than a sham.

This confusion concerning the extent to which the Council and the Assembly adhere in practice to the unanimity rule appears to result from attempts to draw conclusions without resort to a full or detailed study of the practice of these organs. In general, it seems fair to say that conclusions upon the subject have been based upon little more than a study of the language of the Covenant and an attempt to deduce therefrom the practice which is followed by the League. (Attention must be directed to the following notable exceptions: Walther Schücking and Hans Wehberg,

Die Satzung des Völkerbundes, Dritte Auflage, I, 507-522; Jean Ray, *Commentaire du Pacte de la Société des Nations,* pp. 221-236; John Fischer Williams, " The League of Nations and Unanimity," in *American Journal of International Law,* XIX, 475.) Obviously, an accurate picture of the practice can not be gained by such a method. The meaning assigned to rules of law can not always be ascertained by an examination of the language of those rules, particularly when such rules form part of the fundamental law of an actively functioning organism such as the League of Nations. Forces have been at work which have driven the practice far from that which would seem to be implicit in the language of the Covenant. The nature and the importance of these changes can only be ascertained by a study of the practice of the Council and of the Assembly. It is the writer's purpose to set forth in this volume the results of such a study together with an analysis of the effect of the rule upon the functioning of the Council and the Assembly of the League of Nations.

The writer is greatly indebted to Professor W. W. Willoughby of The Johns Hopkins University for profit derived from his stimulating lectures on the jurisprudence of the League of Nations and for his friendly counsel. He also wishes to express his appreciation of the helpful advice tendered him during the preparation of this study by Associate Professor James Hart of The Johns Hopkins University, and by Dr. Frederick Sherwood Dunn, Associate Member of the Walter Hines Page School of International Relations and Creswell Lecturer in International Law. Both Dr. Dunn and Dr. Hart read the entire manuscript, saving the writer from numerous errors both in form and in substance. The writer is also deeply indebted to Professor George Bernard Noble of Reed College for suggesting to him the subject as one which would repay study, for arousing his interest in it, and for directing his very early efforts. Miss Hermione Riches assisted in the preparation of the manuscript for the printer and Professor H. H. Lloyd of Goucher College generously assisted in proof reading.

C. A. R.

CONTENTS

CHAPTER I

The Unanimity Rule in the Plans for the League Covenant

The first two paragraphs of Article 5 of the Covenant of the League of Nations read as follows:

Except where otherwise expressly provided in this Covenant, or by the terms of the present Treaty, decisions at any meeting of the Assembly or of the Council shall require the agreement of all the Members of the League represented at the meeting.

All matters of procedure at meetings of the Assembly or of the Council, including the appointment of Committees to investigate particular matters, shall be regulated by the Assembly or by the Council and may be decided by a majority of the Members of the League represented at the meeting.

Consideration of the forerunners of this article as they may be seen in those plans for a League constitution which had a direct bearing upon the Covenant itself, and consideration of the evolution through which this article passed in the League of Nations Commission and in the Plenary Sessions of the Versailles Conference will throw some light, it is believed, upon the nature of the forces responsible for placing the article in the Covenant, and upon the meaning which the framers believed to be contained in the two paragraphs.

No attempt will be made here to describe the numerous schemes for a League of Nations that were put forward by societies and by individuals prior to the Versailles Conference. It is true, of course, that the League of Nations concept had been widely discussed. Without doubt many of these plans served to crystallize the ideas in the minds of the framers of the Covenant, and some of them probably supplied articles which found their way more or less directly into the draft conventions which served for the interchange of views among those later to be charged with the preparation of the Covenant.

For the purposes of this study, the Phillimore Draft will be used as a point of departure, chiefly because it was the first definite plan for a League of Nations formulated under the direction of a government. Furthermore, it was directly responsible for the preparation of the House Draft, which in turn influenced directly the subsequent Wilson drafts. Moreover, the Phillimore plan likewise influenced the various British drafts which were to follow; and, as will be noted below, the Hurst-Miller Draft, which formed the basis for the discussion in the League of Nations Commission, was a composite of American and British plans.

The Phillimore Draft Convention was prepared by a committee of legal experts, called " The Committee on the League of Nations," appointed by the British government early in 1918. The document takes its name from the chairman of the committee, Sir Walter G. F. Phillimore. In the committee's Interim Report, which they directed to Mr. Balfour, Foreign Secretary at that time, they stated quite frankly that they had attempted to select the best from the practice of nations and from the earlier schemes for creating a permanent international conference and arbitral tribunal.[1] No doubt exists regarding their attitude toward the problem of unanimity, for the report contains the following:

The next questions which enter into consideration in Articles 7, 19, 11, and 12 are whether the decisions of the Conference must be unanimous, and whether, if any resolutions may be passed by a

[1] The Interim Report is printed in full in D. H. Miller, *The Drafting of the Covenant*, I, 4.

majority, the voting strength of the states should differ. We have concluded to eliminate the states parties to the dispute, but the precedents in favor of unanimity are so invariable [2] that we have not seen our way to give power to a majority, or even a preponderant majority, to issue a definite recommendation, though we are aware that many English writers express themselves in a contrary sense. On the other hand, we have felt that for all preliminary work the vote of a majority should be sufficient. We may add that we have been loath to frame a scheme under which our own country should be rendered liable to have a recommendation passed against it by a majority vote in a matter vitally affecting the national interests, and that we have also felt that if some of the enemy Powers are ever to come into this League they would equally be unwilling to submit themselves to such a liability. As to the question of voting strength in cases where a majority is to determine, most English and American writers have contemplated giving a larger vote to the more important Powers, and there are precedents, such as the General Postal Union Treaty of 1878 and the Telegraphic Convention of 1897, for giving to those Powers which have important colonial possessions additional votes in respect of their colonies; but the experience obtained during the Hague Conference of 1907 shows that any such superiority would be greatly resented by some states, and we have shrunk from providing it.[3]

Thus, the Phillimore Committee deemed it wisdom to commit the League to the doctrine of unanimity, except in matters of a procedural character.[4] The latter provision, which is found in Article 7 of the Phillimore Draft, bears some resemblance to Article 5, paragraph 2, of the League of Nations Covenant. Article 7 of the Phillimore draft reads as follows:

The Conference shall regulate its own procedure, and may appoint Committees to enquire and report. In all matters covered by this

---

[2] This, it will be noted, is not strictly accurate in view of the decisions taken at the Hague Peace Conferences by "quasi-unanimity."

[3] Miller, I, 6.

[4] The text of the Phillimore Draft did not specifically require unanimity, but the terms of Article 7 by which exception was made for matters of procedure implied it and the terms of the Interim Report left no doubt.

Article the Conference may decide by the votes of a majority of the Allied States represented.[5]

In July, 1918, the British Government sent copies of the Phillimore Draft to President Wilson and to the Dominion Premiers. The draft was submitted by Wilson to Colonel House with the request that House draw up a plan embodying their own ideas on a league constitution. House was assisted in this work by David Hunter Miller, and their work was completed July 16, 1918. As he worked, House had before him a copy of the Phillimore Draft, but, as he wrote to President Wilson, he did not use it as a basis of his own draft, although in the process of revision he did incorporate several of its important provisions.[6] This is apparently what happened in the case of House's Article 9, for it is nothing other than the Phillimore Article 7 with a sentence inserted. Thus Article 9 of the House Draft read as follows:

The Delegates shall regulate their own procedure and may appoint committees to inquire and report. The Delegates shall constitute a Secretariat and fix the duties thereof and all expenses of the Secretariat shall be paid by the Contracting Powers as the Delegates may determine. In all matters covered by this article the Delegates may decide by the votes of a majority of the Contracting Powers represented.[7]

Nowhere in the House Draft is unanimity specifically required. The implication is, of course, that, if majority voting has to be especially provided for matters of procedure (including finance), unanimity is requisite for other decisions. However, in House's Article 13 and in his Article 20, the latter containing the germs from which were to come Articles 10 and 19 of the Covenant of the League of Nations, liberal

[5] Miller, II, 4.
[6] Charles Seymour, *The Intimate Papers of Colonel House,* IV, 23.
[7] *Ibid.,* IV, 30.

departures from unanimity were made. Article 13 provided that on the request of one of the parties arbitral decisions might be set aside by three-fourths vote of the Delegates if the decision had been unanimous. In the case of arbitral decisions rendered by majority vote, a two-thirds vote of the Delegates was to suffice.[8] Article 20 read as follows:

The Contracting Powers unite in several guarantees to each other of their territorial integrity and political independence, subject, however, to such territorial modifications, if any, as may be necessary in future by reason of changes in present racial conditions and aspirations, pursuant to the principle of self-determination and as shall also be regarded *by three-fourths of the Delegates* as necessary and proper for the welfare of the peoples concerned; recognizing also that all territorial changes involve equitable compensation and that the peace of the world is superior in importance and interest to all questions of boundary.[9]

These provisions for decisions by majorities of two-thirds and three-fourths of the Delegates, particularly the provisions of Article 20, seem to indicate that Colonel House appreciated fully the difficulties which might flow from strict adherence to the doctrine of unanimous consent, and that he was by no means entirely committed to it.

Prior to the transmittal of the Phillimore Draft to President Wilson, the Committee appointed by the French Government to examine conditions on which might be founded a League of Nations had reported. It is not entirely clear whether this report, dated June 8, 1918, had reached House and Miller before they drew up the House Draft. Miller states that the text of the French Draft came before him some time in the summer of 1918.[10] The French Draft was silent

[8] *Ibid.*, IV, 32.
[9] *Ibid.*, IV, 35. Italics added by present writer.
[10] Miller, I, 10.

2

on whether voting would be by majority or unanimity, but from the general tenor of the plan and from its emphasis on sovereignty, it seems safe to surmise that it was intended that all decisions be reached by unanimous agreement.[11] While this draft probably did not influence the House Draft or the First Wilson Draft, the Americans and British were undoubtedly familiar with it before their later drafts were prepared. As noted above, Miller saw it some time during the summer, and the Phillimore Committee prepared a summary of it dated August 9, 1918.[12]

The House Draft was sent to Wilson together with a letter of explanation on July 16, 1918, and it served as a basis for the First Wilson Draft of the Covenant. House's Article 9, which he had taken from the Phillimore Article 7 after inserting a sentence relating to the Secretariat, was carried over by Wilson as Article 2. Some changes in wording were made, Wilson's Article reading as follows:

> The Body of Delegates shall regulate their own procedure and shall have power to appoint such committees as they may deem necessary to inquire into and report upon any matters which lie within the field of their action.
>
> They shall organize a Secretariat to act as their ministerial agency, and the expense of maintenance of the Secretariat shall be borne as they may prescribe.
>
> In all matters covered by this Article the Body of Delegates may decide by a majority vote of the whole Body.[13]

The House provisions of Article 20 were carried over in substance in Wilson's Article 3, and those of House's Article 13 in Wilson's Article 5.

[11] R. S. Baker, *Woodrow Wilson and the World Settlement*, III, 152, gives an English translation of the French draft.

[12] Miller, I, 10.

[13] *Ibid.*, II, 12.

Wilson carried this first draft to Europe but upon his arrival there he was confronted with two new drafts, both dated December, 1918, one by General Smuts, and one by Lord Robert Cecil. Both drafts impressed him considerably. That of Smuts is of particular interest in connection with the question of unanimity. The draft was called " A Practical Suggestion " and did not consist exclusively of articles for a constitution but included considerable comment and explanation. His plan visualized the creation of a general conference in which all states would be represented on the basis of strict equality and the creation of a smaller council in which the great powers would predominate. The general conference would have power to discuss such matters as might be laid before it by the council and would only be able to pass resolutions in the form of recommendations. Smuts does not state whether these should be passed by majority vote or by unanimous consent. On the other hand, the council was expected to take decisions which would create definite legal obligations, and in this body the great powers were to predominate. Decisions could be taken provided not more than two states opposed. In other words, slightly more than a two-thirds majority of the council would be sufficient for a binding decision on any subject within the competence of the League. In defense of these portions of his plan, Smuts wrote in part as follows:

But while we avoid the super-sovereign at the one end, we must be equally careful to avoid the mere ineffective debating society at the other end. The new situation does not call for a new talking shop. We want an instrument of government which, however much talk is put into it at one end, will grind out decisions at the other. We want a league which will be real, practical, effective as a system of world-government The scheme which I have seen, and which brings representatives of all independent states of the world together in conference to discuss the most thorny of all subjects and requires that their decisions to be binding must be unanimous, is from that point of view not worth discussion. It means that there never will be any decisions issuing from the league; that nobody will take the league seriously; that it will not even serve as camouflage; that it will soon be dead and buried, leaving the world worse than it found it.[14]

Such were the views of Smuts on the requirement of unanimity which had been used in many of the " political " conferences prior to the World War. On the problem of equality, Smuts wrote as follows:

The League will include a few great Powers, a large number of small states. If in the councils of the league they are all to count and vote as of equal value, the few Powers may be at the mercy of the great majority of small states. It is quite certain that no great Power will willingly run such a risk by entering a league in which all have equal voting power. Will Great Britain be prepared to put her fleet at the mercy of a ̍ majority vote of all the other states who are members of the league? The question need only be put to see what the answer must necessarily be. The league is therefore in this dilemma, that if its votes have to be unanimous, the league will be unworkable; and if they are decided by a majority, the Great Powers will not enter it; and yet if they keep out of it they wreck the whole scheme. Clearly neither unanimity nor mere majority will do. Neither will it do to assign different values to the states that are members of the league. If Guatamala counts as one, what value shall be given to the United States of America? Will it be five, or ten, or one hundred or one thousand? Will the valuation proceed on the basis of wealth or population or territory? And if either of the last two bases is adopted, what about the powers who have millions of barbarian subjects or millions of square miles of desert territory? . . . . But clearly there is no good reason to be assigned in favor of any basis of valuation, and the principle of values will not help us at all. We therefore proceed to look for some other solution of our difficulty.

The solution Smuts found was the creation of the general conference in which equality was maintained, the conference having power only to recommend,

14 *Ibid.*, II, 38.

and the creation of a council in which the great Powers constituted five of the nine members. He clearly assumes that majority action would be preferred in the interests of efficiency even in this small council if there were not the danger of a decision injuring seriously the susceptibilities of a considerable minority. Thus he writes:

As a further safeguard for the Great Powers and small states alike, it might be laid down that no resolution of the council will be valid if a minority of three or more members vote against it; in other words, more than a two-thirds majority will be required to pass any resolution in the council. This limitation will prevent the council from passing a resolution against which there is a strong feeling, while it will not, I hope, substantially impair the working efficiency of the council. Should a step considered necessary by the majority be vetoed by a minority of three or more, nothing will be left but for the Powers to negotiate among themselves in regard to the removal of the deadlock, and with a certain amount of goodwill a way out will generally be found.[15]

In the Lord Robert Cecil Draft of December, 1918, cited above, no mention is made of whether voting should be by majority or by unanimous consent. However, in view of his championing of unanimity in the meetings of the League of Nations Commission, in the Plenary Sessions of the Versailles Conference, and later in both the Assembly and the Council of the League of Nations, it can scarcely be doubted that he had unanimity in mind.[16]

The influence of the Smuts Draft is clearly perceptible in the Second Wilson Draft (First Paris Draft), January 10, 1919. The Smuts general conference with its power to recommend was taken over almost verbatim, as was the council composed of nine members, five Great Powers, and four representing

[15] *Ibid.*, II, 42.
[16] See below, pp. 17, 21, 27, 214.

two classes of smaller states. It is of particular interest to note that Wilson retains the provision that "three or more negative votes in the Council shall operate as a veto upon any action or resolution proposed."[17] Apparently Wilson agreed with General Smuts that a requirement of unanimity would seriously impair the working efficiency of the Council. Territorial readjustments by a three-fourths vote of the Delegates is retained in this draft from his earlier one.[18] However, while the Delegates are still given power to regulate their own procedure no mention is made in this draft of the majority essential for that action. It will be recalled that, in the Phillimore Draft, the House Draft, and the First Wilson Draft, the conference was to have power to regulate its own procedure by majority vote. No changes in respect to the matters here mentioned were made in Wilson's Third Draft (Second Paris Draft), January 20, 1919.[19]

On the same date, January 20, 1919, another British Draft appeared, which followed in general the lines of the Phillimore Draft and that of Lord Robert Cecil. This draft retained as Article 8 the provisions permitting the Conference of the League to decide questions of procedure by majority vote, with the additional provision that this also apply to the Council.[20] However, the Smuts suggestion of a veto by three or more members of the Council was not adopted, the supposition being that one negative vote in that body would be sufficient to block any decision other than one concerning matters of procedure. In this connection it should be stated that Miller reports an informal meet-

[17] Article 2 of Second Wilson Draft, printed in Miller, II, 65.
[18] Article 3.
[19] Printed in Miller, II, 98.
[20] Printed in Miller, II, 106.

ing being held January 30, 1919, between Wilson, House, Signor Orlando, and Signor Scialoja. Miller notes that

Signor Orlando did not find the idea of giving three votes the power of veto upon any action of the Council practical. To illustrate his meaning he gave the case of an internationalized railway: supposing that a State, through which this railway passed, imposed exorbitant tariffs and refused to alter them at the request of its neighbors, all action could be paralyzed if three adverse votes prevented the Council from reaching a decision.[21]

Orlando, then, was prepared to go even further than Smuts and Wilson in order to establish a council which could not be deadlocked by a minority.

At a conference of Wilson, Smuts, Cecil, and House in the latter's rooms in the Hôtel de Crillon, January 31, 1919, it was decided that Sir Cecil Hurst, British legal adviser, and Miller, legal adviser to the American delegation, should be charged with reconciling, in so far as possible, the British and American texts. The conference between Hurst and Miller resulted in a text known as the Hurst-Miller Draft, which later was used as the basis of discussion in the League of Nations Commission. In this draft the English point of view in regard to voting may be said to have prevailed. The last paragraph of Article 2 retained the provision permitting the Body of Delegates to decide matters of procedure by majority vote, but this did not apply to the Council, as it had in the British Draft of January 20, 1919. In the Hurst-Miller Draft the paragraph read as follows:

All matters of procedure at meetings of the Body of Delegates, including the appointment of committees to investigate particular matters, shall be regulated by the Body of Delegates, and may be decided by a majority of those present at the meeting.[22]

---

[21] Miller, I, 66.
[22] The Hurst-Miller Draft is printed in R. S. Baker, III, 144.

However, the veto by three or more members of
the Council, which provision Wilson had taken over
from the Smuts Plan for his own Second and Third
Drafts, disappeared, as did the guarantee article with
its provisions for territorial changes when agreed to
by three-fourths of the Delegates. It should be noted
that the provision taken from an earlier Wilson Draft
to allow non-members to come into the League by a
two-thirds vote was retained.[23]

President Wilson received a copy of the Hurst-
Miller Draft on February 2, 1919. Miller reports him
far from satisfied. He maintained that many things
had been taken out, some of which he regarded as
being of great importance.[24] Wilson immediately set
to work and produced his Fourth Draft (Third Paris
Draft) using the Hurst-Miller Draft and his own
Third Draft as a basis. In this draft it is significant
to note that Wilson accepted the omission of his
guarantee article but that he persisted in retaining
the veto by three or more members of the Council.[25]
He again included the provision permitting the Body
of Delegates to regulate its own procedure but failed
to state what majority would be necessary for this
action. This latter provision occurs in much the same
form in his Second, Third, and Fourth Drafts. Immediately after the preparation of Wilson's Second
Draft, Miller had called attention to his failure to
specify the vote necessary for the regulation of procedural questions by the Body of Delegates.[26] Wilson's

[23] Article 6. R. S. Baker, III, 146. (Article 12 in Second and Third
Wilson Drafts.)

[24] Miller, I, 72.

[25] Article 2, Fourth Wilson Draft, in Miller, II, 145.

[26] See D. H. Miller, " Comments and Suggestions to Wilson on his
Second Draft." Printed as Doc. 7 in Miller, II, 65.

persistent omission of the provision for majority decision by the Delegates in matters of procedure after
once having accepted it (First Draft), taken with his
belief that the Council should not be hampered by the
unanimity requirement, may indicate a belief that all
decisions by the Body of Delegates should be by
majority unless there was a statement to the contrary.
This view is further strengthened by Wilson's specific
requirement of unanimity for the reduction of armaments made in Article 4 of his first three drafts.

The Fourth Wilson Draft was printed by February
3, 1919, and it was the desire of Wilson to lay it before
the Commission on the League of Nations on that day
as the basis for discussion.[27] However, Wilson was
persuaded that it would be better to place an Anglo-
American proposition before the Commission rather
than one of purely American origin. Hence, the Hurst-
Miller draft was submitted.

Although it is true that the plans advanced by delegations other than those of Great Britain and the
United States had little or no direct effect upon the
Covenant, it seems essential, in order to familiarize
ourselves with the ideas that were in the minds of the
members of the Commission on the League of Nations,
to give brief attention to them. Several of these plans
contemplated a general conference or council or both
in which decisions carrying legal obligation would be
taken by something less than unanimity. The Italian
scheme provided for a conference in which each state
would have one vote, with decisions taken by a two-
thirds majority.[28] The Swiss project provided for a
Council of Mediation in which unanimity would not be

27 Seymour, IV, 301.
28 Florence Wilson, *Origins of the League of Nations Covenant,*
Appendix I.

required. A Conference of States might admit new states to the League by a simple majority vote, each state having one vote, and by a majority of population, each state casting the vote of its entire population, except that no state be allowed to count more than one hundred million. Certain amendments to the constitution might be adopted by a simple majority, others requiring a two-thirds majority.[29] The German scheme contemplated a Congress of States, each state having from one to three votes, with decisions taken by a two-thirds majority.[30]

On the other hand, the French scheme, as already noted, undoubtedly looked for unanimous decisions, as did that submitted by the Scandinavian block—Sweden, Denmark, and Norway.[31]

These continental schemes reflect without doubt something of the idealism of their authors, who were not in all cases " practical statesmen." Nevertheless, these schemes were put forth as serious proposals and in several cases had the endorsement of government commissions. When it is recalled that the drafts of Smuts and Wilson contemplated serious modifications of unanimity and that Signor Orlando favored an even greater modification, it can readily be seen that it was by no means the " visionary scholars " alone who feared that the League would lack working efficiency if committed to strict unanimity. Obviously, the view was held also by some who might be described as " practical statesmen."

[29] H. W. V. Temperley, *A History of the Peace Conference of Paris*, VI, 455.
[30] *Ibid.*, VI, 457.
[31] *Ibid.*, VI, 456.

CHAPTER II

THE INCORPORATION OF THE UNANIMITY RULE IN THE COVENANT

On January 25, 1919, the Preliminary Peace Conference passed a resolution providing for the appointment of a Commission representative of the Associated Governments to work out the details of the constitution and functions of the League of Nations.[1] The Commission was originally expected to have two representatives from each of the five Great Powers, and five representatives of the smaller states. At a meeting held January 27, 1919, Belgium, Brazil, China, Portugal, and Serbia were chosen to represent the latter. The personnel of the Commission was strong, including as it did several heads of delegations and several of those individuals who had been most active in devising schemes for a league of nations.[2] Later, owing to the dissatisfaction of the small states, their representation was increased from five to nine, Greece, Poland, Rumania and Czechoslovakia being awarded the additional seats.[3] President Wilson acted as chairman at all but one of the fifteen meetings of the Commission. At the tenth meeting, Wilson was absent and Lord Robert Cecil presided.

The Hurst-Miller Draft, as noted above, was agreed upon as the basis for discussion in the Commission.

[1] Temperley, VI, 434.
[2] The personnel may be found in the *Minutes* (*English*) of the *Commission on the League of Nations.* Printed in Miller, II, 229, as Doc. 19.
[3] Temperley, VI, 434.

15

The method followed was, in general, to discuss this draft article by article, considering amendments whenever they were suggested. It will be recalled that this draft made no provision for majority action except in Article 2, paragraph 4, which provided that the Body of Delegates might determine matters of procedure by a majority vote; Article 6, which provided that new members could be admitted to the League by a two-thirds vote of the Body of Delegates; and Article 13, which provided that in case of a dispute, the Council, failing to reach unanimity, might issue recommendations to the disputants based upon the findings of the majority. Changes of some importance were, however, brought about in the course of the Commission proceedings.

Article 2, paragraph 4, came before the Commission for consideration at its second meeting, held February 4, and was adopted without opposition. However, an amendment was suggested by Lord Robert Cecil and accepted by the Commission allowing the Executive Council as well as the Body of Delegates to settle matters of procedure by a majority vote. The words " or the Executive Council " were inserted immediately following the words " Body of Delegates." [4] The drafting committee of the Commission changed the paragraph from Article 2, paragraph 4, to Article 4, paragraph 1, the position it occupied in the Covenant adopted by the Plenary Session of the Peace Conference on February 14, 1919.

It can not be doubted that, in the opinion of some and, perhaps, most of the members of the Commission, this paragraph meant that in all other cases, unless specific statement to the contrary was made, the Body

[4] *Minutes (English) of the Second Meeting of the Commission on the League of Nations.*

of Delegates and the Executive Council must decide by unanimous vote. At the Second Meeting of the Commission, Cecil had mentioned that there was great danger in voting if decisions did not require unanimity and great difficulty if they did. For that reason, he introduced the amendment to Article 2, paragraph 4, mentioned above.[5] At another time in the course of the same session, in objecting to M. Vesnitch's (Serbia) proposal that the small states be allowed greater representation on the Council, Cecil said that since the Council was to act by unanimity, to increase its size would make the task of reaching decisions just that much more difficult.[6] That Wilson did not believe the article to imply that all other decisions would have to be taken by unanimity seems clear from a discussion which occurred during the third session of the Commission. The question arose in a further consideration of M. Vesnitch's proposal to increase the size of the Council. Smuts stated that a point made by Wilson was " academic, since the decisions by the Executive Council must be unanimous." Wilson replied that it did not so appear from the text of Article 3. Cecil said: " It is implicit in the article. All international decisions must by the nature of things be unanimous." [7]

Article 6 of the Hurst-Miller Draft, providing for the admission of new members by a two-thirds majority of the Body of Delegates, ran the gauntlet of Commission consideration, coming out greatly changed in wording as Article 7 of the Draft of February 14, 1919. At one point an attempt was made by the French delegation to change the requirement from two-thirds

[5] Miller, I, 140.
[6] *Ibid.*, I, 147.
[7] From notes of Mr. Shepardson. Printed in Miller, I, 161.

of the Body of Delegates to unanimity. M. Bourgeois spoke as follows:

This Article provides admission by two-thirds vote of the Body of Delegates. An important question is raised by this provision. It strongly seems to me that in case of the admission of a new state, it should be by unanimous vote. There should be no doubt left as to the character of the new member. That member should be without reproach. However important it may be to introduce the condition of self-government, the moral test is the true and final test, and unanimity should be the measure.[8]

The French amendment was not accepted. Later Wilson proposed that the Body of Delegates have power to admit new members by a simple majority but his amendment was withdrawn.[9] The withdrawal can be attributed to opposition coming chiefly from the French delegation.[10]

Article 13 of the Hurst-Miller Draft, with its provision for a majority recommendation if unanimity could not be obtained in the Council, came through as Article 15 of the Draft of February 14, 1919. At the fifth meeting of the Commission, M. Hymans (Belgium) attempted to put through an amendment that would have given legal effect to a decision of a majority of the Council. He suggested that, in the second paragraph, the words " if the report is agreed to by the majority of the members " be substituted for the words " if the report is unanimously agreed to by the members " and that the last sentence of the paragraph be replaced by " if the report is unanimously agreed to by the Council other than the parties to the dispute, the High Contracting Parties agree that they will carry out in good faith the decision that has been rendered." [11] M. Hymans received the support of the

[8] *Ibid.*, I, 164.
[9] Florence Wilson, p. 24.
[10] Miller, I, 286.
[11] *Minutes (English) of the Fifth Meeting of the Commission.*

French delegation and that of M. Vesnitch (Serbia) and M. Venizelos (Greece). Cecil, supported by Wilson, opposed. M. Venizelos suggested that a compromise amendment be worked out by which mandatory effect might be given a decision of a majority of the Council, provided that it included a large majority of both large and small states. Cecil persisted in his opposition and the proposed amendment was withdrawn.[12]

At the eighth meeting of the Commission, February 11, 1919, Lord Robert Cecil proposed the addition of an article providing for the amendment of the Covenant. His proposed new article read as follows:

> Amendments to the constitution and functions of the League can be made by an unanimous vote of the Executive Council confirmed by a majority of the Body of Delegates.[13]

M. Venizelos (Greece) said that while he believed it should not be made too difficult to amend the Covenant, he objected to the bare majority requirement in the Body of Delegates while requiring unanimity in the Executive Council. M. Vesnitch (Serbia) suggested that amendments be adopted by the unanimous vote of the Executive Council and two-thirds of the Body of Delegates. M. Venizelos (Greece) and M. Pessoa (Brazil) said that they still preferred a three-fourths majority in the Body of Delegates. They were supported by M. Rolin-Jaequemyns, who had replaced M. Hymans (Belgium). President Wilson then read the following text for the article:

> Amendments to this Covenant will take effect when ratified by the States whose representatives compose the Executive Council and by three-fourths of the States whose representatives compose the Body of Delegates.[14]

---

[12] Ibid.
[13] Minutes (English) of the Eighth Meeting of the Commission.
[14] Ibid.

The text as read by Wilson was adopted as Article 24. Obviously the article as worded by Wilson can be construed in a very different way from the article as worded by Cecil. It does not appear from the minutes that any notice was taken of this at the time by Wilson, Cecil, or any other member of the Commission. It should be noted that the form in which Cecil's amendment was introduced and the subsequent debate leaves little doubt as to the intention of the framers to require majority action of some kind in the *proposal* of amendments rather than in their ratification. As a matter of fact, neither the English minutes nor the French show that ratification was even discussed at the time. Apparently, after some of the small states had shown dissatisfaction with the provision for action by a bare majority in the Body of Delegates, Wilson proposed his wording and it was adopted without debate. From the context of the debate before Wilson offered his amendment, it seems probable that he was thinking of ratification in the sense of approval by three-fourths of the votes in the Assembly, including all represented on the Council, rather than ratification by three-fourths of the governments. However, it should also be noted that the present Article 5, paragraph 1, was placed in the Covenant *after* the provision for amendment. The drafting committee changed this article, adopted as 24, to Article 26 in the Draft of February 14, 1919.

No other changes in respect to voting were made by the Commission in its first ten meetings held before the Covenant was submitted to the Plenary Session, February 14, 1919. In summary, the Hurst-Miller Draft which was submitted to the Commission contained precisely three provisions which specifically permitted action by less than the entire Council or

Body of Delegates. These were the settlement of matters of procedure by a majority vote of the States represented at the meeting of the Body of Delegates, the admission of new members by a two-thirds vote of the Body of Delegates, and provision for a recommendation by a majority of the Council in accordance with the provisions of Article 13 (Article 15 of the Draft of February 14). The Commission added two additional provisions for action by a majority. The Council as well as the Body of Delegates was permitted to settle its matters of a procedural character by a majority vote, and amendments could be adopted when ratified by a three-fourths majority vote of the Body of Delegates including all the members of the Council. The attempt made by Belgium to substitute a majority decision for a unanimous decision of the Council and also to create a legal obligation under the terms of Article 13 (Article 15 of the Draft of February 14) failed, as did the attempt of France to change the provision for the admission of new members from a two-thirds majority of the Body of Delegates to unanimity.

The report of the Commission on the League of Nations was presented to the Plenary Session of the Peace Conference on February 14, 1919. The draft of the Covenant was read by President Wilson, and speeches in explanation and support by Wilson, Cecil, Orlando, Bourgeois, and others followed. Concerning the question of unanimity, Cecil spoke as follows:

Secondly, we have laid down, and this is the great principle in all action, whether of the Executive Council or the Body of Delegates, except in very special cases and for very special reasons which are set out in the Covenant, all action must be unanimously agreed to in accordance with the general rule that governs international relations. That that will, to some extent, in appearance at any rate, militate against the rapidity of action of the organs of the League, is undoubted but, in my judgment, that defect is far more than com-

3

pensated for by the confidence that it will inspire that no nation, whether small or great, need fear oppression from the organs of the League.[15]

That the interpretation given by Cecil was quite generally accepted in Great Britain and continental countries seems evident from resolutions passed at the Inter-Allied League of Nations Conference held in London from March 11 to March 13, 1919. The resolutions show also that it was the view of many that the departures from unanimity in the Covenant should be more numerous. The sixth resolution passed by the Conference was as follows:

> The requirement of unanimity in the Body of Delegates and the Executive Council may result in rendering the League impotent at the will of a single State. It is, therefore, expedient to provide some means for insuring that the majority of the League shall not be debarred by the dissent of a small minority from acting on behalf of the League.[16]

However, many persons in the United States were less willing that the League be constituted in a fashion to permit action by a majority. They were likewise unwilling to trust to the interpretation placed on the Covenant of February 14 by Cecil to prevent this very thing from happening. American opinion on the League seems quite generally to have demanded, together with many other changes, a specific provision in the Covenant to the effect that the unanimity rule would be followed except where the Covenant specified otherwise. For instance, Elihu Root's views were summarized for the American delegation in a dispatch dated March 19, 1919, as follows:

> D. That the provisions as to voting needed clearing up; that if the proposed organs of the league were merely international con-

---

[15] *Plenary Session of the Peace Conference,* February 14, 1919. Printed in Miller, II, 557, as Doc. 23.

[16] Printed in C. A. Kluyver, *Documents on the League of Nations,* p. 309.

ferences the rule as expressed by Lord Robert Cecil in his speech, that unanimity was required except where the contrary was provided, might prevail. However, it was not clear from the instrument whether the bodies created would merely be conferences or whether the league would be a union or even a confederation and that it might well be argued that questions would be decided by majority vote except where the contrary is specifically stated.[17]

On March 18, 1919, ex-President Taft cabled Wilson suggesting that certain amendments to the Covenant be made in order to make secure its acceptance by the Senate. " Require expressly unanimity of action of Executive Council and Body of Delegates " appears as one of the suggestions.[18] This suggestion by Taft was repeated in his cable of March 29. To his words of March 18 he added: " The unanimity of the Executive Council, the American representation on it, will secure reasonable distribution of burdens for the United States in enforcement of Article 10 and Article 16." [19]

Charles E. Hughes in a speech before the Union League Club of New York on March 26 suggested seven amendments to the Covenant. The first of these was " explicit provision of the requirement of unanimity in decision." [20]

In his cable to the American delegation of March 18, Mr. Lamont made an effort to summarize the views of certain leading American newspapers on the Covenant. He noted that the New York *World* was suggesting eleven changes in the Covenant—among them, " that it should be explicitly provided that decision is to be unanimous except where the contrary is stated." [21]

[17] Miller, I, 299.
[18] Baker, I, 324.
[19] Miller, I, 382.
[20] *Ibid.*, I, 383.
[21] *Ibid.*, I, 388.

Other less intelligent expressions of opinion touched on the same question. Senator Capper of Kansas in an article in the Topeka *Daily Capitol* wrote: " I shall decidedly oppose any arrangement to permit foreign nations by a majority vote of the representatives in the League to say when this country shall send American boys, and how many, to fight on a European battlefield." [22] In summarizing the views of the Chicago *Tribune,* Lamont stated that their first objection to the Covenant was that it " creates a world state in which America is a junior partner liable to be outvoted." [23]

On the other hand, some opinion in America held that not sufficient provision was made for majority voting in the Covenant. For instance, William Jennings Bryan suggested certain changes in this direction, stating, however, that he was willing that the Covenant be adopted as it stood in order that the golden opportunity not slip away. He wrote:

I venture to point out certain amendments that should, in my judgment, be made in the interest of a stronger and better League. First, the basis of representation is not fair to the United States. A comparison of voting strength will show that while our nation is the most powerful in the combination, whether measured by population, wealth or moral influence, it has no larger vote than nations much inferior in population, wealth, and influence. This inequality ought, if possible, to be corrected, for justice is the only foundation upon which any institution can rest in permanent security.

Second, the terms of admission to nations that may desire to join hereafter are not fair. To require a two-thirds vote to admit a new nation suggests the social club, where a few blackballs may keep out an uncongenial applicant. This World League is for the world. The President has well said that our nation is not interested in a league unless all nations are in it.

---

[22] *Ibid.,* I, 386.
[23] *Ibid.,* I, 386.

The qualification for admission ought to be fixed, and then it ought to be made as easy as possible for those who are qualified to gain admission. Under no circumstances should the consent of more than a majority be required for the admission of any qualified nation.[24]

Wilson left America for France on March 5, and soon thereafter the League of Nations Commission undertook the task of altering the Covenant so that it might conform to American opinion. At an informal meeting of Wilson, House, Cecil, and Miller on March 18, Cecil agreed to the inclusion in the Covenant of a provision stating that decisions in both Council and Assembly should be taken by unanimous vote except where otherwise provided. Indeed, Cecil had understood from the first that decisions were to be taken in this fashion and he had no objection to putting it in words in order that American opinion might be satisfied.[25]

At the Eleventh Meeting of the Commission, held March 22, Cecil, in accordance with the agreement reached at the informal meeting of March 18, introduced the following amendment to Article 4 of the Covenant:

Except where otherwise expressly provided in the present Covenant, decisions at any meeting of the Body of Delegates or of the Executive Council require the agreement of all the States represented at the meeting.[26]

At the meeting of March 18, they had contemplated omitting the final words " at the meeting " in order to assure absolute unanimity. However, they decided against it as it would have allowed a single state by its absence, deliberate or otherwise, to block all action

24 *Ibid.*, I, 375.
25 *Ibid.*, I, 285.
26 *Minutes (English) of Eleventh Meeting of the Commission.*

by the Council or Assembly.[27] In introducing the
amendment, Cecil again explained that it was " merely
a specific statement of a fundamental principle of the
League; but that its statement would clear away many
apprehensions." [28] The amendment was adopted as
Article 4, paragraph 2. The French minutes, however,
show that some of the members of the Commission
found the amendment a little disturbing. M. Bourgeois
(France) suggested that, in view of the London resolution, careful consideration should be given to the
cases in which a majority vote would suffice. M. Venizelos (Greece) said that he proposed to submit an
amendment in respect to this when Article 15 came
before the Commission for discussion. M. Reis (Portugal) also called attention to the illogical arrangement of the Article as amended. The first paragraph
expressed the exceptions to the general rule and the
second paragraph the general rule.[29] At the Fourteenth
Meeting of the Commission, April 10, M. Reis moved
that the order of the paragraphs be reversed and his
motion was carried. Owing to other changes in the
Covenant, the article had then become Article 5.

As a further indication of Cecil's view that the
addition of the amendment would in no way change
the procedure to be followed in voting, and of his
belief that this view was generally held by his colleagues on the Commission, a statement made by him
at the Fourteenth Meeting may be quoted. Wilson,
with the active support of Cecil, was attempting to
persuade the French delegation to agree to a clause
stating that the validity of the Monroe Doctrine was

[27] Miller, I, 285.
[28] *Minutes (English) of the Eleventh Meeting of the Commission.*
[29] *Minutes (French) of the Eleventh Meeting of the Commission.*

not affected by anything in the Covenant. Wilson had been maintaining that the insertion of the proposed provision relating to the Monroe Doctrine would in no way change the obligations of the United States and that it would not change the interpretation to be given anything in the Covenant. Bourgeois' reply to this was: " Then why put it in the Covenant? " In answer Cecil drew the following analogy:

Perhaps M. Bourgeois will permit me to explain again what I thought was quite clear by this time. In Article 5 we inserted a clause saying that the decisions of the Assembly and of the Council must be unanimous unless otherwise provided for.

All of us felt that there could be no question about this principle but there had been so much misunderstanding about it, that it seemed best to make a definite reference to it. Similarly this amendment proposes to make another implicit principle perfectly clear, that the validity of the Monroe Doctrine is not affected by anything in this Covenant.[30]

No other changes were made in Article 5 during the course of its consideration by the League of Nations Commission. However, at the Plenary Session of April 28, an amendment to the text of Article 5, proposed by Wilson, was adopted. The words " or by the terms of this Treaty " were inserted, making paragraph 1 of Article 5 read as follows:

Except where otherwise expressly provided in this Covenant or by the terms of this Treaty, decisions at any meeting of the Assembly or of the Council shall require the agreement of all the Members of the League represented at the meeting.[31]

This change in the text of Article 5 was made necessary by the provisions in the Treaty of Versailles by which the Council can in certain cases act by majority vote. The subsequent incorporation of the Covenant in three other treaties of peace, all providing certain

[30] Notes of Mr. Shepardson. Miller, I, 445.
[31] *Minutes of Fifth Plenary Session of April 28, 1919.*

cases in which a majority decision of the Council suffices, makes the expression in the Covenant technically inaccurate. The article should read " by the terms of the present treaties," since there are four of them.

At the meeting of the Commission held March 26, Cecil suggested that the amending clause (Article 24) be changed by deleting " three-quarters " and substituting " a majority." This change was made although Venizelos (Greece) who had been largely responsible for the change from a majority to three-fourths of the Body of Delegates raised some objection. Cecil defended his amendment by saying that " it had been represented to him from many quarters that the necessity of amendments being carried by a three-quarters majority would give the League too rigid a character. He considered that the amendment would make no great difference, but that it would remove the impression which existed that the Covenant was to be unalterable." [32] This statement by Cecil throws more light upon the intention of the framers of the Covenant in regard to the proposal of amendments. If they intended only to permit amendments to the Covenant when proposed by a unanimous vote of the Members, to take effect when ratified by a majority of the States members of the League, including all in the Council, the League Covenant would certainly have remained rigid in character; but if they intended that the amendments be proposed as well as ratified by a majority, including all members of the Council, much of the rigidity would be avoided. Unless Cecil expected amendments to be voted by the latter method his remarks in the Commission were quite absurd.

At the Eleventh Meeting of the Commission held March 22, President Wilson made an effort to get the

[32] *Minutes (English) of Thirteenth Meeting of the Commission.*

provision in Article 7 (Article 1 of the final text), which required a two-thirds majority of the Assembly for the admission of new members, changed to a simple majority. Because of the opposition of Bourgeois, however, he withdrew his suggestion. Nevertheless, at the same meeting, a change was made which permits the Council, with the approval of a majority of the Assembly, to name additional permanent members of the Council or to increase the number of members of the League to be selected by the Assembly for the other Council seats (Article 4, paragraph 2). This provision was no doubt inserted in order to provide for increasing the number of permanent members at a time when Russia or Germany might be prepared to enter the League. The provision that the Council might, with the approval of a majority of the Assembly, increase the number of temporary members of the Council was, of course, put into the Covenant out of deference to the small states. The thought that, by use of this provision the balance in favor of the great powers would be upset, does not appear to have been seriously entertained by any of the members of the Commission on the League of Nations.[33]

One other provision for majority decision was inserted in the Covenant by the Commission. At the Twelfth Meeting, March 24, Cecil proposed on behalf of the Greek delegation the following addition to Article 15:

The Executive Council may, in any case under this Article, refer the dispute to the Body of Delegates at the request of any party to the dispute, provided that such request be made within 14 days after the submission of the dispute to the Council. In this case, a recommendation made by the Body of Delegates shall have the force

---

[33] See *Minutes (English) of the Eleventh Meeting of the Commission.*

of a unanimous recommendation by the Executive Council, provided that such recommendation is supported by all the States represented in the Executive Council and a majority of the other States represented in the Body of Delegates.[34]

The amendment was accepted. However, the wording was changed and the text was broken into two paragraphs by the Drafting Committee, the paragraphs finally reading as follows:

> The Council may in any case under this Article refer the dispute to the Assembly. The dispute shall be so referred at the request of either party to the dispute, provided that such request be made within fourteen days after the submission of the dispute to the Council.
>
> In any case referred to the Assembly, all the provisions of this Article and of Article 12 relating to the action and powers of the Council shall apply to the action and powers of the Assembly, provided that a report made by the Assembly, if concurred in by the Representatives of those Members of the League represented on the Council and of a majority of the other Members of the League, exclusive in each case of the Representatives of the parties to the dispute, shall have the same force as a report by the Council concurred in by all the members thereof other than the Representatives of one or more of the parties to the dispute.[35]

It is important to note that the Drafting Committee inserted the words " exclusive in each case of the representatives of the parties to the dispute." The amendment suggested by Cecil had made no such provision. The Drafting Committee also reported another change of somewhat the same character in Article 15, suggesting that the following paragraph be inserted:

> If the Council fails to reach a report which is unanimously agreed to by members thereof, other than the representatives of one or more parties to the dispute, the Members of the League reserve to themselves the right to take such action as they shall consider necessary for the maintenance of right and justice.[36]

---

[34] *Minutes (English) of the Twelfth Meeting of the Commission.*
[35] Article 15, paragraphs 9 and 10.
[36] *Minutes (English) of the Fifteenth Meeting of the Commission.*

The paragraph was adopted and became paragraph 7 of the present Article 15 of the Covenant. The provision for quasi-unanimity, that is, unanimity not including the parties to the dispute, is again included. One other such provision had been in the Covenant throughout the deliberations of the Commission. Article 15, paragraph 6, provides that if a report by the Council is unanimously agreed to by the members other than the parties to the dispute, the members agree not to go to war with any party to the dispute that complies with the recommendations of the report. A provision of this nature was made in the Hurst-Miller Draft, Article 13, paragraph 2, and it was retained in the Covenant of February 14, as Article 15. Indeed, the Article can in substance be found in the Phillimore Plan and several of the subsequent schemes for a League of Nations. The Drafting Committee was not, therefore, introducing a new principle but rather was quite logically providing that the same sort of unanimity should be designated in paragraph 7 as in paragraph 6. However, the report of the Drafting Committee called forth what was apparently the only discussion during the sessions of the Commission of the principle of excluding parties to the dispute from the vote. The discussion is reported as follows in the English minutes:

Mr. Orlando pointed out the difficulties which might arise from the provision that representatives of all the parties to the dispute were to be excluded from the deliberations. There were certain cases where the exclusion of interested parties would lead to most unfortunate results. Suppose a dispute relating to the use of an international canal; if the parties to the dispute were debarred from voting it might happen that small powers not directly interested would settle a question upon which the Great Powers were divided.

Lord Robert Cecil explained the relation of this Article to such an issue. If a dispute were submitted to the Council, the parties to the dispute would participate in the discussion together with other members of the Council. If all the States participating in the discussion should agree upon a unanimous report, no difficulty would arise. On the other hand, should the decision not be unanimous, it would be necessary to exclude the interested parties who were not willing to support the opinion of the majority.

President Wilson said that a state would have to declare either that it was a party to the dispute, in which case it could not vote; or that it was not a party to the dispute, and in that case it could vote.[37]

The principle of excluding interested parties was again observed in the last minute addition of a paragraph to Article 16, reading as follows:

Any member of the League which has violated any covenant of the League may be declared to be no longer a Member of the League by a vote of the Council concurred in by the Representatives of all *other* Members of the League represented thereon.[38]

Thus in Article 15, paragraphs, 6, 7, and 10, and Article 16, paragraph 4, interested parties are not to be counted in reckoning the vote of the Council or Assembly, as the case may be. Three of these four paragraphs were inserted at the last meetings of the Commission while the other had been in the draft of the Covenant throughout its consideration by the Commission. Why the principle was applied in the paragraphs here enumerated and not in such as Article 10; Article 11; Article 13, paragraph 4; Article 15, paragraph 8; Article 16, paragraph 2; and Article 17 has been a subject for considerable speculation. Was the omission in the latter cases deliberate in order to emphasize the need for strict unanimity? If so, several articles of the Covenant were drafted by a Commission

---

[37] *Ibid.*

[38] The paragraph was not in the Covenant of February 14, but appeared in the final draft. Neither the English nor the French minutes show how it got there.

whose members knew that the articles being drafted were devoid of all meaning. The Commission debates and the subsequent utterances of various members of the Commission do not bear out this interpretation.[39] Was it merely a careless oversight that the Covenant, as two members of the Commission have since stated, failed to exclude parties to a dispute from participating in the vote in all cases in which the Council acts in a judicial capacity? However, the minutes indicate that the significance of the principle of not allowing members to sit as judges in their own cause was appreciated when Article 15, paragraph 7, was under discussion in the Commission. The explanations which have been offered and the interpretations of the articles that have been made by the various League organs will be the subject for detailed consideration below.[40]

One other change providing for majority decision appears to have been made by the Drafting Committee, a committee which perhaps might more accurately be described as a committee of revision. At the Eleventh Meeting of the Commission Lord Robert Cecil had suggested the insertion of the following clause:

The first Secretary-General of the League shall be the person named in the protocol hereto and his successors shall be chosen by the Body of Delegates on the nomination of the Executive Council.

This provision appears in the following form as Article 6, paragraph 2, in the Covenant as finally adopted:

The first Secretary-General shall be the person named in the Annex; thereafter the Secretary-General shall be appointed by the Council with the approval of the majority of the Assembly.

[39] See below, pp. 134-135.
[40] See below, pp. 134-157.

Neither the English nor the French Minutes reveal when or by whose initiative this change was made to permit action in this case by a majority of the Assembly. The supposition is that the change was made by the Drafting Committee.

To summarize, it may be said that Article 5, paragraph 1, requiring unanimity in the Council and in the Assembly unless specifically stated to the contrary, went into the Covenant to satisfy American opinion, or more accurately, in an attempt to reconcile a sufficient number of the League's opponents in the Senate to allow consent to ratification. In the view of Cecil, who had more to do with the actual drafting of the Covenant than any other individual, with the possible exception of Wilson, the League was actually committed to unanimity before the Article was inserted in the Covenant. The fact that these expressions of opinion by Cecil never brought forth a real denial by any member of the Commission may indicate that they were all in agreement on this point. However, judging from the drafts submitted by Wilson, Smuts, House, Orlando, and others of the Commission, it seems certain that at the outset they hoped to create a new world organization which could act in some cases, at least, without receiving the express consent of the representatives of each government having membership in the League. The failure of the veto by three members of the Council, that had been provided for in the Smuts Draft and in the second, third, and fourth drafts of President Wilson, to survive in the Hurst-Miller Draft must have served as a warning to them that a Covenant with such provisions could not be accepted by all at that time. It then, no doubt, seemed best to them to avoid mention of how decisions were to be reached so that the League, when it came into being, might not be hampered in evolving by slow process from the atomistic concept to one in which new modes of collective action could be adopted. However, the publication of the Covenant of February 14, and the comment and criticism which followed made it only too clear that American acceptance could not be hoped for without an express provision in regard to unanimity. Immediately after the adoption of Article 5, paragraph 1, there followed numerous attempts to provide exceptions to the general rule so that the League might possess some working efficiency. The delegates had awakened to the need of express exceptions to the rule of unanimity. As has been noted, some of these attempts to insert exceptions were successful and some were futile. Quite possibly the exceptions to unanimity so inserted constituted the extreme limit to which the powers were willing to go at that time.

The reception accorded the Draft of February 14, in countries other than the United States, seems to indicate that it was quite acceptable to them without the express provision for unanimity. They seemed quite willing to accept Cecil's statement at its face value. Instead of agitating for an article giving expression to the views of Cecil, they were more concerned with urging the insertion of the proper exceptions to the principle of unanimity. It seems reasonable to conclude, therefore, that the Covenant would have been just as widely ratified without Article 5, paragraph 1, as with it. Would the subsequent history of the League have been different if this futile attempt to placate American opponents of the League had not been made? Speculation on this subject is perhaps idle, but the present writer is tempted to advance the view that the omission of the Article would not have greatly altered the evolution through which the League has passed. It seems probable that it would have made it somewhat easier for exceptions to the rule of unanimity to have been devised in practice. However, it is submitted that, in spite of Article 5, paragraph 1, the representatives sent by the powers to the Assembly and Council have shown a remarkable ingenuity in avoiding the restrictions of that article where it seems expedient to do so. On the other hand, it has, on occasion, been convenient to adhere to it strictly when an element of danger seemed involved in the pursuit of any other course. The chief obstacle to majority decision is not so much the rule itself as the resistance that stands behind the rule in the form of a recognition of advantages that may flow from its maintenance, bolstered up by juristic concepts that no longer fit the facts of international life. The rule will be modified, even though its language remains the same, wherever and whenever there is a general recognition that the efficient regulation of common interests demands it. In the pages which follow, the attempt will be made to show how far the League has strayed from strict adherance to the rule which appeared to be so strongly entrenched at the beginning.

CHAPTER III

MODIFICATIONS OF UNANIMITY ACHIEVED THROUGH PRACTICE

It has been pointed out above that the League of Nations Covenant provides that, except where expressly provided to the contrary in the Covenant or by the terms of the peace treaties, decisions of the Assembly or Council require unanimous vote. In the Covenant the stipulated exceptions to the general rule of unanimity were as follows:

1. Article 1, paragraph 2, providing for the admission of new members to the League by a two-thirds vote of the Assembly.

2. Article 4, paragraph 2, providing that the Council may name additional permanent members of that body with the approval of a majority of the Assembly. The same paragraph likewise provides that the temporary membership of the Council may be increased by the same vote.

3. Article 5, paragraph 2, provides that all matters of procedure at the meetings of the Assembly or Council, including the appointment of committees to investigate particular matters, shall be decided by a majority vote of those present.

4. Article 6, paragraph 2, provides that the Secretary-General shall in the future be appointed by the Council with the approval of a majority of the Assembly.

5. Article 15, paragraph 4, provides that if a dispute is not settled by arbitration or by the mediation of the Council, the Council, either unanimously or by ma-

jority vote, shall make and publish a report containing a statement of the facts of the dispute and the recommendations which are deemed just and proper in regard thereto.

6. Article 15, paragraphs 6 and 7, provide that if a report of the Council is unanimously agreed to by the members of the League other than the representatives of one or more of the parties to the dispute, the members of the League agree not to go to war with any party to the dispute which complies with the recommendation. It is recognized that if the Council fails to reach such a unanimous agreement, exclusive of the parties, the members of the League reserve to themselves the right to take such action as they shall consider necessary for the maintenance of right and justice.

7. Article 15, paragraph 10, provides that, when disputes are referred from the Council to the Assembly, a report of the latter body concurred in by those members of the League represented on the Council and a majority of the other members of the League, exclusive in each case of the parties to the dispute, shall have the same force as a unanimous report of the Council, exclusive of the parties.

8. Article 16, paragraph 4, provides that, should a member violate any covenant of the League, it may be excluded from the League by a vote of the Council concurred in by the representatives of all the other members of the League represented on the Council.

9. Article 26, paragraph 1, provides that amendments to the Covenant take effect when ratified by the members of the League whose representatives compose the Council and by a majority of the Members of the League whose representatives compose the Assembly.

That concludes the list of specific exceptions to the rule of unanimity found in the Covenant as it was adopted. It might be added, however, that a most important departure was made from the rule when provision was made for a Council composed of five permanent members and four temporary elective members. Since the Council has certain special functions which it can deal with without any action on the part of the Assembly, the great majority of the states members of the League are deprived of their customary *liberum veto* on certain classes of cases.

In the Peace Treaties drawn up at Versailles, St. Germain-en-Laye, Neuilly-sur-Seine, and Trianon between the Allied and Associated Powers and Germany, Austria, Bulgaria, and Hungary respectively, certain other provisions were made for majority decisions being taken by the Council. It will be remembered that, at the Plenary Meeting of April 28, Wilson had moved an amendment to Article 5 in order to make the article state that decisions would be unanimous except where otherwise expressly provided in the Covenant or by the terms of the present treaty.[1] The amendment was adopted. Consequently, the following treaty provisions form exceptions to the general rule of unanimity prescribed in Article 5, paragraph 1.

The Treaty of Versailles provides that decisions on questions relating to the Saar Valley be taken by majority vote of the Council. Article 50 reads as follows:

The stipulations under which the cession of the mines in the Saar Basin shall be carried out, together with the measures intended to guarantee the rights and well-being of the inhabitants and the government of the territory, as well as the conditions in accordance with which the plebiscite hereinbefore is to be made, are laid down in the Annex hereto. This Annex shall be considered as an integral part of the present Treaty, and Germany declares her adherence to it.

---

[1] See above, p. 27.

Section 40 of the above mentioned Annex to Article
50 provides:

> In all matters dealt with in the present Annex, the decisions of the
> Council of the League of Nations will be taken by a majority.

The treaties provide that the Council may give directions for the investigation of the compliance of the
Central Powers with the disarmament provisions of
the treaties and that such directions may be issued
by a majority vote of the Council. Thus Article 213 of
the Versailles Treaty reads as follows:

> So long as the present Treaty remains in force, Germany under-
> takes to give every facility for any investigation which the Council
> of the League of Nations, acting if need be by a majority vote, may
> consider necessary.

Similar provisions are found in the treaties with
Austria, Hungary, and Bulgaria.[2]

In respect to the treatment of minorities, The Treaty
of St. Germain with Austria provides:

> Austria agrees that the stipulation in the foregoing Articles of this
> Section, so far as they affect persons belonging to racial, religious
> or linguistic minorities, constitute obligations of international concern
> and shall be placed under the guarantee of the League of Nations.
> They shall not be modified without the assent of a majority of the
> Council of the League of Nations. The Allied and Associated Powers
> represented on the Council severally agree not to withhold their
> assent from any modification in these Articles which is in due form
> assented to by a majority of the Council of the League of Nations.[3]

Similar provisions are found in the treaties of peace
with Hungary and Bulgaria.[4]

The significance which may be attached to these departures from unanimity will be discussed below.

---

[2] St. Germain, Article 159; Trianon, Article 143; Neuilly, Article
104.

[3] Article 69, paragraph 1.

[4] Trianon, Article 60, paragraph 1; Neuilly, Article 57, paragraph 1.

It may then be said that the League of Nations came into being committed to the general rule of unanimity that had become accepted in the diplomatic practice of the preceding century, tempered to some extent by those exceptions to the principle that have been noted. Although some scholars deplored the failure of the authors of the Covenant to create an international body in which the majority could bind the minority,[5] it was more generally conceded that they were wise to have adopted the accepted mode of taking decisions.[6] To some critics, the exceptions to the rule of unanimity seemed to be of some considerable importance, while others could see little in them. Indeed, this latter belief still persists to a considerable degree. If one bases one's view solely upon the wording of the Covenant one will quite logically arrive at such a conclusion. However, the League Covenant can no more be interpreted strictly by its language than can, for instance, the Constitution of the United States. Both have evolved and will continue to evolve. The League has already moved a very considerable distance from the strict unanimity that seems to be implicit in the words of the Covenant.

Article 5 has in general been interpreted by the organs of the League of Nations in a manner that removes from that article much of its rigor. The language would appear to one unfamiliar with League procedure to require the unanimous approval of all members of the Council or Assembly represented at the

[5] See F. B. Sayre, *Experiments in International Administration* p. 153.

[6] See D. W. Morrow, *The Society of Free States,* p. 167; Temperley, VI, 451; Baker, "The Making of the Covenant," in Rask-Orstedfonden, *Les Origines et l'Oeuvre de la Société des Nations,* II, 66.

meeting for each decision other than one of a procedural character, including the appointment of committees to investigate. Such is not in fact the case. These changes have been accomplished by the interpretation given by the League organs to the words of the article, an interpretation which tempers them to a marked degree.

ABSTENTIONS

It will be recalled that, when the Commission on the League of Nations was considering the wording of Article 5, it was suggested at one time to omit the words " represented at the meeting " in order that absolute unanimity might be required. However, this suggestion was not adopted, it being felt that decisions should not be blocked by the inadvertent or deliberate absence of a member. Both the Council and the Assembly have moved still further beyond the principle of strict unanimity and have decided that the unanimity requirement is satisfied even though a resolution is not voted for by all the members present at the meeting. Those members unable to express an affirmative vote may abstain from voting without defeating the resolution. Provision to this effect was made by Article 19 of the Assembly Rules of Procedure adopted by the First Assembly. The Article reads as follows:

1. Except where otherwise expressly provided in the Covenant or by the terms of a treaty, decisions of the Assembly shall be taken by an unanimous vote of the Members of the League represented at the meeting.

2. All matters of procedure at a meeting of the Assembly including the appointment of committees to investigate particular matters, shall be decided by a majority of the Members of the League represented at the meeting.

3. All decisions taken in virtue of these Rules shall be considered as matters of procedure.

4. A majority decision requires the affirmative votes of more than half of the Members of the League represented at the meeting.

5. For the purposes of this Rule, Representatives who abstain from voting shall be considered as not present.[7]

It will be noted that this has the effect of preventing an abstention from defeating a resolution which requires unanimity and that it also permits, in matters that can be decided by majority vote, the taking of decisions by a majority of those voting. In the Second Assembly M. Rolin (Belgium) explained the adoption of the provision to count those who might abstain as absent as follows:

I must remind you of the reasons which led us to adopt this rule last year: it was a means of avoiding the obligations of unanimity. It was not desired that the indifference or hesitation of certain members on a question in which the unanimity of the other members was certain should hinder a vote if a member considered that he was not justified in making use of his right of opposition where unanimity was required, and it was admitted that he might abstain without invalidating the vote.[8]

Thus when the Assembly was faced with the necessity of achieving unanimity, a point was stretched to make it somewhat less difficult. Those who abstained might be said to have given tacit approval to the action of the Assembly. Although M. Rolin found no fault with the decision to count abstentions as absences in cases in which the League was obliged to achieve unanimity, he did not consider the same provision proper when a majority vote would suffice for a decision by the Assembly. In the same speech in which he defended the practice where unanimity was essential, he suggested

[7] *Rules of Procedure of the Assembly* (1920), p. 7, and *ibid.* (1931), p. 9.

[8] *Records of the Second Assembly,* Plenary, p. 731.

that it be changed where only a majority vote was required. He spoke as follows:

> The procedure should be different in the case of a vote by a simple majority. In all the Parliaments of the World, if 60 members vote and 20 abstain, the absolute majority is 31, not 21. Now, according to our Rules of Procedure, the majority on 60 members, if there are 20 abstentions, is 21, and the three-fourths majority, if there are 20 abstentions, would therefore be 30, and not 45.[9]

The suggestion that the Rules of Procedure be changed to prevent this practice was not acted upon and consequently the Assembly continues to take majority decisions counting those who abstain as absent.

The Council as well as the Assembly has held that abstentions do not prevent unanimity although no such provision is to be found in its rules of procedure. Although abstentions are far more unusual in the Council than in the Assembly, the practice of not allowing them to obstruct the achievement of unanimity has been definitely established. At the Tenth Session of the Council, held in 1920, while giving consideration to the language to be employed by the Permanent Court of International Justice, a situation arose which made a ruling on the question imperative. All of the members of the Council, with the exception of M. Bourgeois (France) were in favor of substituting an article of their own creation for Article 37 prepared by the Hague Jurists relating to the language to be employed by the court and before the court. Mr. Balfour (Great Britain) proposed that, when the vote was taken, M. Bourgeois abstain and that such abstention be not interpreted to prevent the Council from passing the resolution. The suggestion was followed with the result that the resolution was reported to have passed without the vote of M. Bourgeois.[10] However, the practice

9 *Ibid.*, p. 732.
10 *Official Journal*, Number 8 (1920), p. 19.

followed in this case received no formal recognition by the Council and does not appear to have been duplicated until several years later.

The question was brought forward sharply in 1926 during the discussions concerning the composition of the Council. Increasing the size of the Council would in all probability make the achievement of unanimity in that body far more difficult. It was important that all means of alleviating this difficulty be explored. The question was brought forward in the first session of the Committee on the Composition of the Council. The Spanish delegate, M. de Palacios, suggested at this time that the principle of unanimity, which the Spanish Government had always supported, would not loom as such a great obstacle to the successful functioning of an enlarged Council if a definite statement could be made on whether unanimity was impaired by an abstention from voting. He suggested that the Assembly practice be adopted by the Council, for it would often happen that a state would be able to content itself with abstaining without preventing unanimity from being reached.[11]

M. Motta (Switzerland), Chairman of the Committee, expressed the view that the question had already been settled in just the way that the Spanish delegate had suggested. The practice had been followed repeatedly in the Assembly and he did not believe that it would be possible to support with valid arguments the proposition that, if abstention did not detract from unanimity in the Assembly, it should do so in the Council. Accordingly M. Motta stated that, under reserve of any more precise information or any further

[11] *Committee on Composition of the Council:* Report on the work of the First Session, p. 24. (League Doc. C. 299. M. 139. 1926. V.)

discussions which should arise, it should be admitted at once as a principle of positive law in respect of the League of Nations that abstention did not prevent unanimity from obtaining.[12] M. Scialoja (Italy) expressed the view that abstention did not prevent unanimity in the Council but that abstentions would necessarily be more rare than in the Assembly.[13] Viscount Cecil (British Empire) said that it was perfectly clear that the rule of the League was that abstention did not affect unanimity.[14] No member opposed this view, although those who opposed increasing the size of the Council might well have deemed it to their advantage to do so.

The importance of the decisions by the Assembly and Council holding that unanimity has been achieved even though some members have abstained can be readily perceived. It permits a member of the Council or Assembly who has vigorously opposed an action that is contemplated to permit that very action to be taken without seeming to buckle under to such an extent as to lose his dignity. Those who find themselves opposed to the course that the majority wish to pursue have two courses of action open to them. They can cast negative votes and so veto the action, or they can show their disapproval by refusing to join in the affirmative vote without incurring the disfavor that may be heaped upon those who prevent the taking of a decision desired by a large majority. For a state to abstain when it is opposed to a resolution can in no way injure national pride. If, however, an opposing state had to vote in the affirmative it might be so interpreted. In short, providing for affirmative and negative votes and abstentions gives those states who find themselves in a

[12] *Ibid.*, p. 26.
[13] *Ibid.*, p. 26.
[14] *Ibid.*, p. 93.

minority a place to go without forcing them to deadlock the Assembly or Council. In the Assembly the right to abstain has been used frequently and, as will be shown below, has been responsible for the passage of many resolutions that must otherwise have failed. In the Council, abstentions have occurred less frequently.

It has sometimes been suggested that a state which abstains and thus permits a decision to be taken may later reconsider and make the decision invalid. This view would hold that an abstention is a reserving of one's vote. Certainly the Assembly rule providing that those who abstain are to be considered absent does not lend weight to this view, and the debate in the Committee on the Composition of the Council indicated their view to be that an abstention was to be considered as tacit agreement to the decision. That the former view is, however, held by some is shown by the action of M. Galvanauskas (Lithuania) in the course of the budget debates in the Sixth Assembly. M. Galvanauskas spoke as follows:

I can not possibly agree to the Committee's proposals. I can not accept the new scale for three years any more than I can accept the number of units allocated to my country. The Lithuanian Government will thoroughly examine this scale. Not wishing, however, to take the responsibility of wrecking the League's budget for this year by opposing the Committee's proposals, the Lithuanian delegation will abstain from voting.[15]

The resolutions proposed by the Fourth Committee were adopted, Lithuania abstaining, and M. Galvanauskas said:

I maintain my former reservation. I do not consider the scale which has been established as binding for my country. My government retains an open mind on the subject.[16]

[15] *Records of the Sixth Assembly,* Plenary, p. 144.
[16] *Ibid.,* p. 145.

The only comment made was a statement by the President of the Assembly, M. Dandurand (Canada) that the Lithuanian delegate's statement would be placed in the record of the meeting.[17]

It is not believed that the reservation made by the Lithuanian delegate could have any legal validity in face of the wording of the Assembly rule and the interpretation later given to the Assembly and Council practice by the Committee on the Composition of the Council, acquiesced in by all. Moreover, such a view would have the effect of holding that a very large number of Assembly decisions could later be made void, as abstention in that body is by no means a rare occurrence. The acceptance of this view would create an intolerable situation and it seems safe to conclude that an abstention will continue to be treated as a tacit agreement rather than as a reservation of one's vote.

While it seems clear that the legal validity of a particular resolution adopted by unanimous vote can not be questioned later by the representatives of a state which abstained, neither can it later be maintained that an abstaining state has definitely committed itself to the principles involved in such a resolution. An abstaining state retains greater freedom than those having cast affirmative votes, for it can not be asserted that it has committed itself upon the principles involved in the resolution. The abstaining state has chosen only to acquiesce in the adoption of a certain resolution rather than to exercise its right of veto. Consequently, should a resolution later appear in which similar principles were involved, it could not be correctly asserted that all had given approval to those principles.

17 *Ibid.*, p. 145.

Neither the Covenant nor the Rules of Procedure of the Assembly fix the number of members that must be present in order that the Assembly transact business. Hence, it is quite conceivable that decisions can be taken by this body without the approval, positively or tacitly given, of some of its members. It sometimes happens that states members of the League fail to send representatives to the Assembly and it frequently happens that all of a state's appointed representatives are absent when the Assembly is in session. The rules of the Council provide that at least a majority of the representatives of the members must be present when a meeting is opened and that a meeting must be adjourned whenever a majority ceases to be present.[18] In practice, members of the Council usually attend. Therefore, there is little opportunity for decisions to be reached by that body without all having an opportunity to participate.

In one case the Covenant clearly requires that more than a majority of the members be present for taking a decision. Article 16, paragraph 4, provides that " any Member of the League which has violated any covenant of the League may be declared to be no longer a Member of the League by a vote of the Council concurred in by the Representatives of all the other Members of the League represented thereon." It would seem, therefore, that, to exclude a Member from the League, all Members of the Council except the representatives of the state to be excluded would have to be present and cast affirmative votes, while in all other cases the Council could act with only a majority present. Thus, aside from decisions under Article 16, paragraph 4, Council unanimity can be satisfied if a majority is present and

---

[18] *Rules of Procedure of Council*, Rule 6.

none casts a negative vote. It seems highly unlikely, however, that the Council would take decisions if many abstained. In the Assembly, unanimity is satisfied when none of those present cast negative votes. But if either the Assembly or the Council had cared to make the unanimity provision in the Covenant strict, it would have been quite possible for them to have done so by providing in their rules of procedure that business is transacted only when all or a large majority are present. Instead, the Council has fixed the quorum at a simple majority and the Assembly has left the matter without regulation.

MATTERS OF PROCEDURE

The provision of Article 5, paragraph 2, of the Covenant to the effect that all matters of procedure at meetings of the Assembly or Council, including the appointment of committees to investigate particular matters, shall be regulated by majority vote of the Assembly or Council, is of more importance than at first might appear. The provision was inserted so that the Assembly and Council would possess some degree of working efficiency and would not have to depend upon the unfailing good will of every member to take every step. Indeed, the rule was expected to make it impossible for a single state to impede the reaching of definite decisions by preventing the application of suitable means of procedure. Had such a provision not been made, a member wishing to prevent a substantive decision could have done so, without assuming responsibility for the action, by simply vetoing the procedural question which quite possibly might arise before a substantive issue could be drawn.

The authors of the Covenant made no attempt to define " matters of procedure " other than to provide that it was to include " the appointment of committees to investigate particular matters." Thus the League was given virtually a free hand to decide what constitutes questions of a procedural character and what constitutes questions of a substantive character. That the line drawn between the two types of questions will have an important bearing upon the extent to which the unanimity rule restricts the League is readily apparent.

The preliminary question concerning the method to be employed by the League organs in the determination of what constitutes a matter of procedure early came to the attention of the Assembly in connection with the selection of the non-permanent members of the Council. The First Committee of the First Assembly submitted a series of five resolutions pertaining to the method of selecting those Members. The Committee *rapporteur,* Mr. Balfour (British Empire), announced that they had not been able to arrive at resolutions that were acceptable to all and, indeed, that the resolutions submitted did not have the support of very substantial majorities.[19] If resolutions on the subject of the selection of the non-permanent members of the Council were to be treated as of substantive character, unanimity would be essential and, apparently, would be very difficult to achieve. On the other hand, if they were treated as matters of procedure, the resolutions could be readily adopted.

The first question facing the Assembly was the method that it should employ in deciding whether these resolutions were procedural or substantive. Two conflicting views were presented on this point, one holding that it would be necessary for some outside authority to interpret the Covenant upon this point, the other,

[19] *Records of the First Assembly,* Plenary, p. 418.

that the Assembly itself was competent to do so, acting by unanimous vote.

Mr. Millen (Australia), champion of the first point of view, spoke as follows:

The discussion upon the last matter which has been submitted for debate points attention to one of the most serious omissions in the Covenant itself, and that is a direction as to what authority is to be called upon to decide whether matters are procedure or whether they are material to the Covenant itself.

It has to be remembered that this Covenant represents for this Assembly what a written constitution does in a federation, and it is not competent for the Parliament of a federation itself to determine whether it is working within the orbit of its constitution or not. In all the constitutions of the kind to which I am referring there is indicated some outside authority to which is remitted disputes that may arise concerning the validity of any action taken by the legislative body. I submit that it is not competent for this Assembly itself to determine what is a matter of procedure or not. If it were competent for it to do so *it would be easy for the Assembly little by little to alter the whole text of the Covenant by simply declaring matter after matter to be merely a matter of procedure.* It is to be regretted that those who shaped the Covenant, owing to the pressure of many events, the shortness of the time, left the omission to which I direct attention. I strongly urge that even if it means a delay of some time, before we attempt to take action by declaring this, that or the other thing to be a matter of procedure, and possibly by doing that, trespass upon the sovereign rights of the sovereign states, even if it means the lapse of another twelve months, we should be careful to see that some authority is constituted, the International Court of Justice for instance, to which matters could be referred when we are in doubt as to whether we are interpreting the Covenant aright or are by breaking it, trespassing on the rights of the individual states.[20]

M. Schanzer (Italy) advanced the view, agreed to by the Assembly, that the Assembly itself was competent to decide such questions:

The question raised is of a subtle and complex nature. It is very important so far as it concerns our procedure on future occasions.

---

[20] *Ibid.,* p. 424. Italics added.

I do not wish to pretend to propose solutions which can be followed, but I do not think I can agree with the theory presented by the Delegate from Australia. He is of the opinion that the Assembly has not the power to take a preliminary decision as to whether the question is, or is not, one of procedure, and he has quoted in support federal constitutions in which a competent tribunal exists to deal with these questions. He has said that our constitution, that is to say, the Covenant, makes no provision for such a tribunal and consequently there exists no authority which can settle this question.

I can not accept the theory of the Delegate from Australia, who is under the impression that the Covenant has created no competent authority to deal with these questions. In my opinion, on the contrary, the Assembly has full power to decide if the question is one of procedure or not.

There is the second question. In what way can it be decided how to find out whether the point at issue is a point of procedure or a question of principle? When the Assembly has been called upon to take a decision, should that decision be unanimous, as has been laid down with regard to decisions on matters of principle, or should it be sufficient to secure a two-thirds vote? I think that a decision taken on the nature of a question raised—that is to say on the question whether it is a point of procedure or not which is under discussion—is not a question of procedure but of principle. Consequently, the decision to be taken must be unanimous.[21]

It might at first appear that the necessity of determining by unanimous vote the preliminary question of whether in fact a question be one of substance or procedure would completely destroy the advantage of being able to decide procedural matters by majority vote. Such in fact is not the case, for precedents are formed which the Assembly and Council feel strongly obligated to follow. On the first occasion on which a particular question arises, it may happen that no member or group of members has any interest in preventing it from being handled by a majority vote. Consequently, it is quite likely to be deemed a matter of procedure. The precedent is then established and, when similar questions

21 *Ibid.*, p. 426.

5

arise, will be followed. On the other hand, when the question, at its first presentation, is considered by some to be procedural and by others to be of a substantive character, the Assembly and Council leaders have shown themselves to be remarkably adroit at avoiding the mistake of allowing the body to decide that the question is substantive. The question therefore remains open and, quite possibly, when it next arises it may not conflict with the self-interest of any member or group of members and can be deemed a matter of procedure. Thus, whenever unanimity can not be achieved for holding a question one of procedure, the League has avoided the mistake of deciding that it is therefore one of substance. They avoid the issue for the time being, return to it at a more opportune moment, and gradually accumulate precedents for treating a surprisingly large number of important subjects as questions of procedure to be settled by majority vote. In the pages immediately following, each subject which has been held by the Council or by the Assembly to be a " matter of procedure " will be discussed.

(1) Both the Assembly and the Council have considered from the first that matters pertaining to the order of the business and the determination of the rules of procedure are matters of procedure subject to settlement by majority vote. The practice, already established, was given definite recognition during the second year of the League's existence. The Netherlands delegation had introduced an amendment to Article 5, paragraph 2, providing that the words " including the Rules of Procedure " should be inserted.[22] The object of this proposed amendment was definitely to establish the rule that modifications of the Rules of Procedure might be made by majority vote. This amendment was

---

[22] *Records of the Second Assembly*, Plenary, p. 690.

referred by the Council, together with others, to the Committee on Amendments to the Covenant and by the Assembly to its First Committee. The Netherlands delegation was persuaded to withdraw its amendment after the Committee on Amendments to the Covenant and the First Committee of the Assembly both had held it superfluous. The Assembly Committee designated it as inadvisable as well as superfluous. The Committee on Amendments to the Covenant reported in part as follows:

This amendment, in addition to making a reference, in the Covenant itself, to the Rules of Procedure adopted by the Assembly at its first Session, also gives express sanction to the provision that amendments to these Rules may be made by the Assembly by a simple majority vote. The Committee is of the opinion that the Rules of Procedure are, without any possible doubt, questions of procedure such as can be settled by a simple majority, in accordance with paragraph 2 of Article 5 of the Covenant. The Committee therefore does not consider it necessary to propose an amendment to the existing text, which it considers to be sufficient to meet the case for which the Netherlands Government desires to provide.[23]

The report made by the First Committee and adopted by the Assembly [24] deserves quotation:

The Assembly rules of procedure were adopted last year by a simple majority vote. An attempt at justifying this procedure, *ex post facto*, by way of an amendment would give rise to a useless discussion on the legitimacy of the method adopted, and would thus risk jeopardising the very result at which the Netherlands Delegation was aiming. There was no doubt that with the text in its present form, the Assembly would adopt any modification of the rules of procedure by a simple majority.[25]

The Rules of Procedure of the Assembly and of the Council, determined by majority vote of the body con-

[23] *Committee on Amendments to the Covenant:* First Report to the Council, p. 13. (League Doc. A. 24. 1921 V.)

[24] *Records of the Second Assembly,* Plenary, p. 853.

[25] *Records of the Second Assembly,* First Committee, p. 179.

cerned, may, of course, provide for special majorities for the determination of certain questions while providing for simple majorities in other cases. However, the Rules of Procedure of both Assembly and Council were themselves adopted by a majority vote of the body concerned and can be so altered.[26]

(2) All decisions relating to individuals are to be deemed matters of procedure, according to the Rules of Procedure of the Council and of the Assembly, and consequently such decisions are taken by majority vote.[27]

(3) The Assembly has not only made its selection of officers by majority vote, but at its first session made the bold decision that the selection of non-permanent members of the Council constituted a " matter of procedure." Article 4, paragraph 1, of the Covenant, which provides for the selection of the non-permanent members of the Council by the Assembly, does not specify the method to be followed beyond providing that they " shall be selected from time to time in its discretion." The First Committee was commissioned by the Assembly to study the problem of how the Assembly should exercise this function granted to it by the terms of the Covenant.

The committee prepared a series of five resolutions on the subject and submitted them to the Assembly for their consideration; the first paragraph of the second resolution and the fifth resolution respectively read as follows:

In execution of Article 4, paragraph 1, sentence 2, of the Covenant, the non-permanent Members of the Council shall be elected one at

---

[26] The Assembly adopted its rules of procedure in the course of its first session (*First Assembly,* Plenary, p. 229). The Council rules of procedure were not adopted until May, 1920.

[27] *Rules of Procedure of the Council,* Rule 9; *Rules of Procedure of Assembly,* Rule 21.

a time and by secret ballot for a period of two years. If no Member obtains at the first ballot an absolute majority of votes, a new ballot shall be taken, but on this occasion the voting shall be confined to the two Members which obtained the largest number of votes at the first ballot. If at this ballot the two Members obtain an equal number of votes, the President shall decide by lot.

The present provisions shall be deemed matters of procedure within the meaning of Article 5, paragraph 2, of the Covenant.[28]

None of the resolutions was carried by unanimous vote in the committee and some were carried by very small majorities. As might be expected, they encountered considerable opposition when submitted to the Plenary Session. The opposition centered chiefly upon the third and fourth resolutions which provided for non-reeligibility and for selection on the basis of geographical location, respectively. Several members, among them M. Schanzer (Italy), M. Benes (Czecho-Slovakia), and M. Usteri (Switzerland), asserted that these resolutions restricted the freedom of choice by the Assembly and hence were matters of substance rather than of procedure. M. Schanzer, for instance, stated that the only question of a strictly procedural nature was that providing for secret ballot.[29] In order to prevent the Assembly from concluding that, since it could not unanimously agree with the committee's decision that the resolutions were of a procedural character, they must therefore be substantive, Mr. Balfour (British Empire), the Committee *rapporteur*, suggested that the last three be deleted and that the second be amended by inserting the words " at the present session." He also suggested that a third resolution be adopted to read as follows :

The various proposals considered by the First Committee of the Assembly on this subject shall be sent to the Committee to be con-

---

[28] *Records of the First Assembly*, First Committee, p. 110.
[29] *Records of the First Assembly*, Plenary, p. 427.

stituted by the Council for studying amendments to the Covenant,
which shall report on them to the next Assembly.[30]

These resolutions were adopted by the Assembly,
establishing the right of that body to name the non-
permanent members of the Council by majority vote.
For the original fourth resolution providing for selection on a regional basis, Mr. Balfour substituted a recommendation, the significance of which from the point
of view of the League's constitutional development will
be considered below. It might be said in passing, however, that substantially the same effect was achieved
by this device as would have been achieved had the resolution as reported by the Committee been adopted.

Additional changes of great importance in the procedure followed by the Assembly in the selection of the
non-permanent members were brought about as a result
of an amendment to Article 4 passed by the Second
Assembly and coming into force July 29, 1926. This
amendment provided that the Assembly have power to
" fix by a two-thirds majority the rules dealing with
the election of the non-permanent Members of the Council, and particularly such regulations as relate to their
term of office and conditions of reeligibility." The First
Assembly had decided that it had power to elect the
non-permanent Members by majority vote, but it had
been unable to decide that regulations relating to the
term of office, regional representation, and reeligibility
were, strictly speaking, matters of procedure. Hence
the amendment was necessary. The significance of the
regulations adopted by the Assembly on September 15,
1926, in pursuance of the power conferred by the
amendment will be discussed below in connection with
a consideration of the changes wrought through formal

[30] *Ibid.*, p. 433.

amendments to the Covenant. The aim here has been to establish the interpretation given to "matters of procedure" by the Assembly and Council and it has been shown that the Assembly held the actual selection of non-permanent members to be a matter of procedure, but that it was unable to hold the fixing of terms, reeligibility, and the representation of geographical areas, which would limit the freedom of choice of future Assemblies, to be of such a character.

(4) Article 5, paragraph 2, confers upon the Assembly and Council the right to settle all matters of procedure "including the appointment of Committees to investigate particular matters" by majority vote. From the wording it is clear that the members of such committees of inquiry may be selected by the Council or Assembly by majority vote, which, of course, gives considerable assurance that competent and impartial persons can be named when the Council or Assembly feels the need for unbiased information before proceeding to the settlement of a dispute. However, if the League organs had stopped at this point in determining the meaning of the words "including the appointment of Committees to investigate particular matters" they would still have found themselves severely hampered in dealing with disputes of a political nature. For if the provision refers solely to *selecting the commissioners* by majority vote, it would seem that a unanimous vote is still necessary, according to Article 5, paragraph 1, for the decision *to set up* the commission of inquiry in the first place. Happily, the League organs have not construed the article in this narrow fashion.

The first declaration to the effect that decisions to establish, as well as the decisions relating to the personnel of committees of inquiry, should be treated as procedural questions was made by a sub-committee of the First Committee of the Second Assembly in a report subsequently accepted by the First Committee. The sub-committee was charged with studying suggested amendments to Article 5 of the Covenant. This necessitated a determination of the meaning of that article as it stood. In respect to what should be considered as constituting " matters of procedure," it was the opinion of the committee that the terms should be construed " in the widest sense." Since the Covenant itself provided that the appointment of committees to investigate belongs to the category of procedural questions, it seemed to the Committee that that must be understood not only as meaning the nomination of members " but also the very establishment of these committees." [31]

The first occasion upon which the clause was put to the test came in connection with the dispute beween Albania and Jugoslavia in 1921, referred by Albania to the League Council under Article 11. On October 2, 1921, the Assembly adopted the following resolution:

The Assembly . . . . requests the Council forthwith to appoint a small Commission of three impartial persons to proceed immediately to Albania, and report fully on the execution of the decision of the Principle Allied and Associated Powers as soon as it is given, and on any disturbances which may occur on or near the frontier of Albania.[32]

When the Council sought to set up the commission in accordance with the terms of the Assembly resolution, M. Boskovitch (Jugoslavia) was willing to cast an affirmative vote, but only subject to reservations. He stated that he accepted the resolution setting up the Commission with the proviso that it should be

[31] *Records of the Second Assembly,* First Committee, p. 179.
[32] *Records of the Second Assembly,* Plenary, p. 660.

clearly understood that the field of its activities should be limited strictly to Albania.[33] The commission did in fact so limit itself. The Council debate at the time of the submission of the resolution to create and instruct the commission of inquiry does not reveal any effort to avoid a negative vote by Jugoslavia. It appears to have been their belief that the commission could be established to operate in Albania even though Jugoslavia's opposition should take the form of a hostile vote. However, no clear precedent can be drawn from this case, unless it be that in similar circumstances a negative vote or a reservation might prevent a commission of inquiry from operating in the territory of the state casting that vote.

In 1922, however, the Council very definitely held that the decision to set up a commission of inquiry to ascertain facts to be used in the settlement of a dispute is a matter of procedure to be settled by majority vote. The question arose in the dispute between Lithuania and Poland referred to the Council by Poland under Article 11 of the Covenant. At the Council meeting of May 17, 1922, M. Hymans (Belgium), *rapporteur,* submitted two resolutions for the approval of the Council. The final paragraph of the first resolution provided that the Council " send to the spot a Commission to study the line which may eventually be adopted and to submit a report to the Council." [34]

M. Sidzikaukas (Lithuania) stated that his government was unable to accept a resolution providing for the appointment of a commission of inquiry to study a new line of demarcation.[35]

[33] *O. J.,* 1921, p. 1193.
[34] *O. J.,* 1922, p. 549.
[35] *Ibid.,* p. 550.

M. Hymans (Belgium) stated "that he was of the opinion that the Council could take a decision despite the opposition of the Lithuanian Representative. It was merely a question of procedure, and in this the Council could take a decision by a majority. The proposed Committee would have no power to take a decision and would have to present a report to the Council." [36]

The Council, following the leadership of its *rapporteur*, treated the matter as one of procedure, and proceeded in spite of the opposition of M. Sidzikaukas (Lithuania) to set up a commission of inquiry.

In the Greco-Bulgar dispute of 1925, the Council placed in one resolution a dictatorial request that within twenty-four hours the parties give orders to their troops to cease fire and withdraw, and also a provision that a commission of inquiry, as requested by Bulgaria, be set up. This commission was to be composed of British, French, and Italian officers. The resolution was first approved in a private session of the Council from which the parties to the dispute were excluded.[37] The representatives of Bulgaria and Greece were then invited to return to the meeting and give their approval. In voting for the resolutions the representatives of the parties to the dispute were signifying their intention to comply with the request. The decision had, in reality, been taken by the Council exclusive of the representatives of the parties to the dispute.

In 1927, the case for establishing commissions of inquiry by majority vote was considerably strengthened by a report made by the Committee of the Council on Article 11 which received the endorsement of both

[36] *Ibid.*, p. 551.
[37] *O. J.*, 1925, p. 1699.

the Council and the Assembly.[38] The committee drew
a distinction between cases in which " there is no imminent threat of war or it is not acute " and those " where
there is an imminent threat of war." [39] In the case of
a dispute falling within the first classification the committee stated:

> If there is a doubt as to the facts of the dispute, a League Com-
> mission may be sent to the *locus in quo* to ascertain what has actually
> happened or is likely to happen. It is understood that such a Com-
> mission can not go to the territory of either party without the consent
> of the state to which that territory belongs.[40]

It will be observed that this follows the precedent
laid down by the Council in the dispute between Albania and Jugoslavia. It in no sense denies that such
commissions can be set up by majority vote but rather
implies that they can be, holding that when the situation is not acute, the state whose territory is to be entered must give its consent. If one negative vote could
prevent such a commission from being established, the
provision here made would be unnecessary.

For cases in which there is an imminent threat of
war the committee recommended the following:

> In order to satisfy itself of the way in which these measures have
> been carried out and to keep itself informed of the course of events,
> the Council may think it desirable to send representatives to the
> locality of the dispute . . . . The Council may also have recourse
> in this connection to diplomatic personages stationed in the neighbor-
> hood who belong to states not parties to the dispute.[41]

Here it will be noted that no provision is made for
gaining the consent of the party whose territory is
to be entered. The decision to establish such a com-

[38] *O. J.,* 1927, p. 764.
[39] *Ibid.,* p. 832.
[40] *Ibid.,* p. 832.
[41] *Ibid.,* p. 833.

mission does not require unanimity. It might conceivably be asserted that the Committee of the Council on Article 11 did not intend that the setting up of a commission of inquiry be treated as a matter of procedure but rather intended to prevent a member sitting as judge in his own case. It is the opinion of the writer that, in view of the statements of M. Hymans and the Council decision in the dispute between Poland and Lithuania, it was their intention that the setting up of a commission of inquiry be treated as a procedural question. It also seems apparent that they desired to establish certain safeguards for national sovereignty in cases in which the situation was not acute. In view of the fact that Article 11 makes no provision for excluding the votes of the parties to the dispute, it would, perhaps, be more damaging to the cause of those who favor strict maintenance of the unanimity rule to adhere to the latter theory—that is, that the committee desired to establish or strengthen the precedent that, in cases arising under Article 11 in which there is an imminent threat of war, the votes of the parties to the dispute are not counted.

In the view of some, the failure of the Council in the Sino-Japanese dispute immediately to set up a commission of inquiry, as it had done in its successful handling of the Greco-Bulgar case in 1925, in spite of Japan's insistence upon direct negotiations, may indicate that the Council does not consider that it can take this step in the face of an adverse vote. Instead of setting up a commission of inquiry in September, as China had desired, the step was not taken until requested by Japan in December.[42] However, it is not believed that the failure to take this action came from a belief on the

[42] *O. J.*, 1931, p. 2365.

part of the Council that such action could not legally be taken without the approval of Japan. The Council sitting in September, 1931, with a personnel which was not regarded as strong, found itself in a difficult position. It was faced for the first time with the necessity of dealing with a great power that was apparently bent on pursuing a course in defiance of the provisions of the Covenant to which it had subscribed. In the Corfu Case the Council had been able to shift its vexatious problem to the Conference of Ambassadors, but in this case there was no such opportunity. The difficulty was further increased by the reports which were circulated concerning assurances given to the Japanese Ambassador at Washington by Mr. Stimson, United States Secretary of State, to the effect that he favored direct negotiations between the two parties and that he would not favor American participation in the work of the proposed commission of inquiry.[43] In short, the Council was tempted to seek a course of action which would be agreeable to Japan and to the important non-Members who were interested in the case. The Council, by following precedents established in earlier cases, could have established a commission of inquiry without the consent of Japan, but it seemed to be more expedient to await a moment at which Japan and the United States would give their approval to such a course. A competent observer attributes to the United States the failure of the Council to take the step suggested by previous practice, summarizing the situation as follows:

The evidence indicates that the normal step of appointing a commission of inquiry would almost certainly have been taken at the outset, even in spite of Japanese unwillingness, if the United States had at that time supported the effort to make this move. American

---

[43] Felix Morley, *The Society of Nations,* p. 442.

indifference, if not opposition, to the step strengthened the Laodicean element in the Council, enabling Japan to block cooperative intervention. In two months' time, after Manchuria had been completely detached from Chinese control, Japan somewhat sardonically proposed the very commission of inquiry which it had at first opposed. The United States then endorsed the step.[44]

(5) Although the Sino-Japanese dispute did nothing to strengthen the view that the establishing of commissions of inquiry as well as the selection of their personnel are to be treated as matters of procedure, it was responsible for the creation of another precedent of great importance; namely, that the Council may by majority vote invite non-Members to attend its meetings. The question arose, of course, in connection with the invitation accorded the United States to sit with the Council.

At the Council meeting held October 15, M. Briand asked the permission of that body to invite the United States to " send a representative to sit at the Council table so as to be in a position to express an opinion as to how, either in view of the present situation or its future development, effect can best be given to the provisions of the Pact." [45] M. Yoshizawa (Japan), however, raised a series of objections to the extension of the invitation. He drew attention to the terms of Article 4, paragraph 5, which provide that League Members may be accorded membership in the Council during consideration of matters specially affecting their interests, and to Article 17, which contemplates invitations being extended to non-members having a direct interest in the dispute. In his view, neither article covered the case. Furthermore, if the United States was to be invited because it was a signatory of the Kel-

[44] *Ibid.*, p. 470.
[45] *O. J.*, 1931, p. 2322.

logg Pact, there was no reason why the Council should not invite all other signatories who were non-members. And, in any case, it was his view that, since the dispute was before the Council under Article 11, a unanimous vote would be necessary in order to extend the invitation.[46]

However, it was the view of the majority of the members of the Council that the question of extending an invitation to the United States was one of procedure to be settled in accordance with Article 5, paragraph 2, of the Covenant. M. Yoshizawa (Japan) suggested that the matter be referred to a committee of jurists for their opinion, but he declined to agree in advance to accept their conclusions.[47] When put to a vote, the proposal to refer the matter to jurists was defeated, only Japan and Germany voting for it.[48] The decision to invite the United States was thereupon taken by a vote of thirteen to one, Japan casting a negative vote.[49] The position of the majority all along had been that they were acting under neither Article 4, paragraph 5, nor Article 17, but were acting in accordance with the terms of a resolution adopted unanimously September 22, 1931, in which the Council had decided to keep the United States fully informed on the progress made in the settlement of the dispute. Hence, they could assert with reason that the substantive question of American participation had already been decided by unanimous vote and that the question whether the United States should be invited to have a representative present at the Council meetings was, therefore, a purely procedural question. They were merely proposing, so they

[46] *Ibid.,* p. 2323.
[47] *Ibid.,* p. 2325.
[48] *Ibid.,* p. 2329.
[49] *Ibid.,* p. 2329.

asserted, a new form of communication with the United States, namely, the substitution of oral for written.[50] Had this earlier decision not been taken, the success of the movement to invite the United States would certainly have been most dubious. The incident did not involve, therefore, a clear-cut decision to the effect that non-members can be invited to participate in Council meetings by a majority vote. The point was somewhat clouded over by the earlier Council decision taken by unanimous vote. However, inasmuch as the decision to invite the United States was taken over the vigorous protest of a great power, it seems reasonable to conclude that the incident will be interpreted as supplying precedent for the addition of non-member states to the Council by the method laid down in the Covenant for settling procedural questions.

(6) Another precedent which may be of some slight importance in determining how the League organs interpret the meaning of " matters of procedure " was established by a Council decision taken in connection with the awarding of contracts for the construction of the buildings of the League of Nations.

On November 19, 1926, the Secretary-General of the League received the following telegram from the Italian Government:

> The shortness of the period fixed for the submission of plans for the competition for the League of Nations building is a handicap also to many Italian architects who have undertaken studies and other work with a view to entering this important international competition. It would therefore be desirable to have the time-limit sufficiently extended. I should be glad if you could arrange for the inclusion of this matter in the next Council agenda—Grandi.[51]

[50] See particularly the letter of the President of the Council, M. Briand (France) to M. Yoshizawa (Japan), dated October 15, 1931, (*O. J.*, 1931, p. 2323) and the remarks of Lord Reading (British Empire) (*Ibid.*, p. 2326).

[51] *O. J.*, 1927, p. 138.

At the Council meeting held December 9, 1926, M. Titulesco (Roumania), *rapporteur*, stated that the Jury of Architects had, at a meeting December 3, decided by majority vote that no change should be made in the rules for or date of the competition. Upon the suggestion of M. Titulesco the situation was explained to the Council by M. Horta, Chairman of the Jury of Architects. The Council thereupon decided that, before adopting any resolution on this subject, it would call upon a committee of jurists to decide whether a resolution on the subject should be adopted unanimously or by majority vote.[52]

At the meeting of the Council held December 9, the Council decided by majority vote to uphold the decision taken by the Jury of Architects.[53] The decision was taken over the negative vote of Italy, a permanent member of the Council. It can, therefore, be expected that questions relating to such matters as the procedure to be followed in the awarding of contracts will always be deemed matters of procedure within the meaning of Article 5, paragraph 2, of the Covenant.

(7) We have now reached a subject in respect to which the League organs have been less bold in defining what constitutes " matters of procedure " within the meaning of Article 5, paragraph 2, of the Covenant, but also one in which they have hesitated to close the matter by a decision to the effect that it is not one of procedure. The point in question is whether the Assembly and the Council must act by unanimous vote or merely by majority in requesting an advisory opinion from the Permanent Court of International Justice. The Covenant is not explicit, merely providing in Article 14 that " the Court may also give an advisory opin-

[52] *Ibid.*, p. 138.
[53] *Ibid.*, p. 152.

ion upon any dispute or question referred to it by the
Council or by the Assembly." Since the Article does not
specify the vote necessary for the request of an advisory
opinion it would be quite possible to hold that, under the
terms of Article 5, paragraph 1, it must, therefore, be
unanimous. On the other hand, it would be equally
plausible to hold that the requesting of an opinion is
nothing other than a matter of procedure to be settled
by a majority vote according to Article 5, paragraph 2.

Perhaps the strongest argument in favor of constru-
ing the terms of the Covenant in such a fashion as to
require unanimity is that, in practice, the procedure followed by the Court in advisory opinions is substantially
like that in cases in which they render decisions impos-
ing legal obligations upon the parties. As a result of
this procedure and because of the great prestige
enjoyed by the Court, advisory opinions are in fact
treated as being virtually as obligatory as judgments.
Hence, if a majority vote suffices for requesting an
advisory opinion, states may in fact be hailed before
the Court without their consent being given.

The view that a majority vote should suffice has been
considerably strengthened by the decision of the Council
to the effect that they can set up commissions of inquiry
by majority vote, for if the Council can by such a vote
decide to set up a special body to supply it with advice
concerning the facts in question or concerning legal
questions which are at issue, it would seem that it
should be able by the same vote to turn to an organ
already in existence for advice on questions of the same
nature. The wording of Article 14 also lends weight to
this view, inasmuch as the provision authorizing the
requesting of advisory opinions is separate and distinct
from that authorizing the Court to render decisions in
cases presented for judgment.

However, neither the Assembly nor the Council has in fact asked the Permanent Court by majority vote for an advisory opinion and neither body has come to a definite conclusion on whether it would be proper to do so. Furthermore, the Court itself has never been called upon to decide whether it would honor a request put to it by a majority vote of the Assembly or Council. Considerable attention has, however, been devoted to the question by both bodies and the Court has on occasion thrown out some statements that might be considered as hints concerning what its attitude would be should the question be placed squarely before it. While no definite position has been assumed by any of the League organs upon the question of whether advisory opinions should be requested by majority or unanimous vote, they have ruled upon several related questions. For instance, it has been quite clearly established that, in certain instances when an advisory opinion is being requested on a dispute before the Council or the Assembly, the votes of the parties to the dispute will not be counted in determining whether the requisite majority or unanimous vote has been achieved. Also it has been established that the Court will not entertain requests for advisory opinions in a dispute in which a non-Member state is a party without the consent of that state.

The question was for the first time thrown open to general consideration and debate in 1926, at the Conference of States Signatories of the Protocol of the Permanent Court of International Justice as a result of the second part of the fifth American reservation to the Protocol. The reservation by the United States was as follows:

Nor shall it [the Court], without the consent of the United States, entertain any request for an advisory opinion touching any dispute or question in which the United States has or claims to have an interest.[54]

The members of the conference believed that this reservation could be attributed to the desire of the members of the United States Senate to put their country on a basis of equality with those states having permanent representation on the Council.[55] It also appeared to be the belief of the Senators that a unanimous vote was required for requesting an advisory opinion and that consequently each of the great powers was armed with a veto which could be used in either Council or Assembly. They were asking such a veto for the United States. This interpretation of the Senate's position was drawn from a speech of Senator Walsh, M. Fromageot (France) quoting him as follows:

" Under the Covenant of the League of Nations, each of the great nations had a representative on the Council of the League; and any one of them therefore, because the Council proceeds by unanimity, can prevent submission to the Court of any request for an advisory opinion with respect to any question concerning which the United States claims an interest." [56]

M. Fromageot suggested, however, that he was by no means certain that the view held by the American Senator was correct. He stated that if the Council's resolution had to be unanimous because a request for an advisory opinion was to be considered a question

[54] *Minutes of the Conference of States Signatories of the Protocol of Signature of the Statute of the Permanent Court of International Justice* (1926), p. 20.

[55] The intention of the Senate had to be inferred, for Secretary of State Kellogg smugly declined the invitation to have an American representative present at the Conference to explain the reservations, stating that they were " plain and unequivocal." See his reply to the invitation printed as Annex 6 to the *Minutes of the Conference*.

[56] *Minutes*, p. 22.

of substance rather than one of procedure, " it was very clear that the United States Government by itself could prevent unanimity being reached unless, to take a more optimistic view, it would consent to the reference to the Court." If, on the other hand,

Article 5 were to be interpreted in the sense that reference to the Court should be regarded as a matter of procedure to assist the Council in forming an opinion on the question submitted to it, leaving it free thereafter to accept or reject the Court's opinion as it thought fit, the Council's resolution would in that case be adopted on a majority vote, and the dispute could be referred to The Hague in spite of the opposition of the United States Government, whose reservation would thus be infringed because, in opposition to the wishes of the United States Senate, the Court would then be giving an advisory opinion without the consent of the United States Government.

M. Fromageot was therefore of the opinion that the first question for the Conference to settle in regard to this reservation was whether the requesting of an advisory opinion from the Court was in fact a matter of procedure or one of substance.

Sir Cecil Hurst (British Empire) drew attention to a circumstance in which, in his view, it had already been settled that all members of the Council did not possess a veto on the requesting of advisory opinions. It was his opinion that when the Council was dealing with a dispute under Article 15 the votes of the parties to the dispute would not be counted in any vote on whether or not an advisory opinion should be requested. This, he stated, was quite apart from whether the decision should be by unanimous vote or majority vote. He believed that his was the only interpretation that could reasonably be drawn from the opinion of the Court in the Iraq frontier case.[57] Hurst was, there-

[57] No member of the Conference challenged this conclusion of Sir Cecil Hurst's.

fore, of the opinion that the United States Senate was, in this case at least, laboring under a misconception when they acted upon the assumption that unanimity was always required for requesting advisory opinions.[58] M. Castberg (Norway) called attention to the fact that, in cases in which the United States was a *bona fide* party to the dispute, the Court would not entertain a request for an advisory opinion without its consent.[59] The Court had, in the Eastern Carelia Case, held by a small majority that it was not proper for the Court to give an opinion in such a case involving a dispute between a member and non-member where the non-member had not signified its consent.

M. Rolin (Belgium) suggested that the Conference recommend that the Council clear up the matter by asking the Court for an advisory opinion upon the subject.[60]

Sir Cecil Hurst announced himself as opposed to the suggestion of M. Rolin. He expressed doubt as to whether the League had advanced sufficiently to make it wise at present to try to obtain an opinion which must to a great extent be regarded as binding for the future. He was not sure that it might not be better to leave the matter in some obscurity and allow the cases with which the Council would have to deal in the future to indicate the correct rule, perhaps by successive opinions given by the Court on disputes or other matters referred to it. It would, in fact, be better to wait for the rule of law to develop out of practical cases rather than to ask the Court to give a binding opinion upon a problem which at present was not ripe for solution.[61]

[58] *Minutes*, p. 24.
[59] *Ibid.*, p. 41.
[60] *Ibid.*, p. 23.
[61] *Ibid.*, p. 24.

The course here suggested by Sir Cecil Hurst has in fact been the one pursued by the League in dealing with this problem. Even though the delegates at this Conference were anxious for the United States to become a signatory to the World Court Protocol, they were unwilling to achieve this gain if it were at the same time necessary to sustain the loss that would come from the adoption of the American view that unanimity is always essential for requesting advisory opinions. The opposition to the acceptance of this American reservation was perhaps most strongly put by Sir George Foster (Canada), who said:

> But this reservation, if adopted without any qualifying clause, would be binding and would hinder the progress of the League in the future; as a result fifty or sixty world nations, upon whom fall the burden and responsibility of carrying on the work of the League, would be unable to modify or change its methods except with the permission of one nation which stood outside, free from all responsibilities, and which naturally was not in sympathy with its work.[62]

None of the delegates present at the conference expressed the view that unanimity was always required for requesting advisory opinions, most of them holding that it was a matter which should be held open or on which they should seek expert legal advice, either from the Court or from a committee of jurists especially designated to study the question. Several expressed the view that, in their opinion, requesting an advisory opinion should always be looked upon as a matter of procedure to be settled by majority vote.[63]

The Final Act adopted by the Conference dealt as follows with this American reservation:

> The second part of the fifth reservation makes it convenient to distinguish between advisory opinions asked for in the case of a dis-

---

[62] *Ibid.*, p. 31.

[63] M. Dinichert (Switzerland), *ibid.*, p. 40, and M. Rolin (Belgium), *ibid.*, p. 38.

pute to which the United States is a party and that of advisory opinions asked for in the case of a dispute to which the United States is not a party but in which it claims an interest, or in the case of a question, other than a dispute, in which the United States claims an interest. As regards disputes to which the United States is a party, it seems sufficient to refer to the jurisprudence of the Court, which has already had occasion to pronounce upon the matter of disputes between a Member of the League of Nations and a State not belonging to the League. This jurisprudence, as formulated in Advisory Opinion No. 5 (Eastern Carelia) given on July 23, 1923, seems to meet the desire of the United States.

As regards disputes to which the United States is not a party but in which it claims an interest, and as regards questions, other than disputes, in which the United States claims an interest, the Conference understands the object of the United States to be to assure itself of equality with states represented either on the Council or in the Assembly of the League of Nations. This principle should be agreed to. But the fifth reservation appears to rest upon the presumption that the adoption of a request for an advisory opinion by the Council or Assembly requires a unanimous vote. *No such presumption, however, has so far been established. It is therefore impossible to say with certainty whether in some cases, or possibly in all cases, a decision by a majority is not sufficient.* In any event, the United States should be guaranteed a position of equality in this respect; that is to say, in any case where a state represented on the Council or in the Assembly would possess the right of preventing, by opposition in either of these bodies, the adoption of a proposal to request an advisory opinion from the Court, the United States shall enjoy an equivalent right.[64]

The Final Act of this conference may be looked upon as an authoritative summary of the practice of the League in respect to the requesting of advisory opinions in so far as it had developed up to 1926.

In September, 1927, the question arose before the Council again in connection with the "Salamis" case in a way that brought forth some clear statements of the position of several of the governments upon the question. The representative of one great power, Italy,

[64] *Ibid.,* p. 79. Italics added.

went definitely on record in favor of holding that the
requesting of an advisory opinion should be considered
as a matter of procedure to be settled by majority vote.
Greece had requested the Council to give a ruling
upon the question whether Articles 190 and 192 of the
Versailles Treaty prohibiting the construction of warships or naval war material in Germany and their
export to foreign countries applied to the construction
of vessels which had been contracted for by German
shipyards prior to the outbreak of the World War.
The dispute was between the Greek Government and
a German firm which wished to fulfill its contract closed
with Greece before the war, providing for the construction of the cruiser " Salamis." Greece desired the Council to ask the World Court for an advisory opinion on
the subject. However, Germany, who was not a party
to the dispute, opposed. The question quite naturally
arose as to whether the request could be made by majority vote. M. Scialoja (Italy) expressed the following
opinion:

> I think that, according to the terms of our Rules of Procedure
> and of the Covenant, a simple majority is enough, because it is a
> question of procedure and we are always free not to accept that
> opinion and thus to remain masters of the situation. Further, the
> matter is one of an act of procedure in regard to a question of pro-
> cedure, for questions of competence belong to the category of the
> larger questions of procedure.
>
> Without insisting on this point, I think that the vote on the request
> for an advisory opinion, especially in the present case, should be
> taken by a majority and not unanimously.[65]

M. Titulesco (Roumania) was unable to accept the
views of M. Scialoja. He spoke as follows:

> If he [M. Scialoja] was referring to a general rule, I feel bound
> to express the exact opposite opinion. An advisory opinion is not
> an act of procedure. By asking for an advisory opinion, the Council

[65] *O. J.*, 1927, p. 1473.

in actual fact ceases to deal with the question and substitutes for itself the Permanent Court in the matter of the decision. It is true that, in theory, the Council is not bound by such an opinion. But in practice, what would happen to the prestige of the Permanent Court of International Justice *proprio motu* if the Council itself asked for an opinion and if it did not consider itself bound by that opinion?

M. Scialoja himself gave us this morning an example of the prestige in which the Court stands, since he extolled the merits of his action in bowing to an opinion which was not quite in conformity with his legal convictions. But there is something more. Suppose an advisory opinion is sent back to the Council. The Council has to vote unanimously in order to take a decision. How is it possible to respect an advisory opinion asked for by a majority vote if the matter has to be decided by unanimous vote?

Since to ask for an opinion is equivalent to ceasing to deal with the question, since the prestige of the Permanent Court is a matter of absolute necessity, since unanimity in taking the decision is indispensable in the Council, and since that unanimity cannot be obtained if the opinion of the Court is asked for by a majority, I must say that, in my view, advisory opinions can only be asked for unanimously.[66]

In evaluating the views of M. Titulesco it should be remembered that his country had since 1923 been engaged in a dispute with Hungary which might well be described as a long drawn out struggle on the part of Roumania to prevent the dispute being referred to the Court for either judgment or advisory opinion. Great weight, therefore, can scarcely be accorded to his expressions of opinion, for they are not those of a disinterested party even though he was technically such in the particular case before the Council.

Additional motive for the hesitancy of the Council in even attempting to act in accordance with the views of M. Scialoja can be seen from the further remarks of M. Titulesco in which he was supported by the Presi-

[66] *Ibid.,* p. 1474.

dent, M. Enriques Villegas (Chile). M. Titulesco spoke as follows:

To lay down as a principle, for the first time in the existence of the League, that it is possible to request an advisory opinion by a mere majority seems to me to be somewhat imprudent, especially when we know that one of the motives for which the great American Republic did not adhere to the Statute of the World Court of International Justice was precisely because it could not be sure that, in asking for an advisory opinion, unanimity was not required. It has not been said that advisory opinions may be requested by a majority vote, it has not been said that they are not requested unanimously, although it has been the constant practice to demand unanimity. To settle such a question today in regard to a special case seems to me to be making final the abstention of the United States, which I consider to be provisional.[67]

The President, M. Villegas (Chile), said:

Despite the respect which the opinion of M. Scialoja deserves, I must say that I greatly hesitate to follow it, because the matter concerns an extremely grave question. As the representative of Roumania has very rightly pointed out, this was the reason why the United States did not adhere to the constitution of the Permanent Court of International Justice. I can not agree with the views of M. Scialoja, nor can I maintain that he is wrong.[68]

The Council thereupon gave up the attempt to refer the question raised by Greece to the Court for an advisory opinion, instead referring it for study to the legal advisers attached to each member of the Council.[69]

In March, 1928, the Council again found itself debating the question of advisory opinions. This time it arose in connection with the later stages of the Hungarian Optants dispute between Hungary and Roumania. The case, which had first arisen in 1923, involved the question whether the Roumanian land laws were in conflict with Article 63 of the Treaty of Trianon.

[67] *Ibid.*, p. 1474.
[68] *Ibid.*, p. 1474.
[69] *Ibid.*, p. 1475.

The dispute had been laid before the Council by Hungary under Article 11, paragraph 2, of the Covenant. The Council, considering it a case suitable for submission to arbitration or judicial settlement, had desired to turn it over to the Court for judgment but was prevented from doing so by the opposition of M. Titulesco (Roumania). The Council then attempted to secure an advisory opinion from the Court, a procedure to which the Hungarian representative readily agreed. Roumania again opposed and the question of whether a decision by majority vote would suffice was not pushed. Having thus failed to gain a judicial settlement by the World Court, Hungary proceeded to act under Articles 239 and 250 of the Treaty of Trianon which conferred on the Mixed Arbitral Tribunal compulsory jurisdiction in cases of claims growing out of the liquidation of ex-enemy properties. Roumania countered this move on the part of Hungary by withdrawing her arbitrator, holding that the tribunal had exceeded its powers. Hungary appealed to the Council to name deputy arbitrators for the Mixed Roumanian-Hungarian Arbitral Tribunal and thus, in 1927, the Council found itself again dealing with the dispute and again in need of legal advice on such questions as whether under Article 239 of the Treaty of Trianon the Council has the duty or only the right to name substitute judges for the Mixed Arbitral Tribunal and whether the Mixed Arbitral Tribunal had in fact exceeded its competence. On this occasion another representative of a state having permanent representation on the Council, Dr. Stresemann (Germany), expressed the view that the question of the vote necessary for requesting advisory opinions should be speedily settled and, furthermore, it should be held that a majority suffices.[70] M. Titulesco

[70] *O. J.*, 1928, p. 429.

(Roumania) replied to Dr. Stresemann in a fiery speech in which he maintained his former position on the necessity of unanimity and in which he charged Stresemann with attempting to circumvent the provisions of Article 14 of the Covenant and bring about compulsory arbitration by majority vote.[71] The Council again refrained from pressing for a decision on the question and so passed a resolution, without securing the advice of the Court, providing that the Council should name two persons, nationals of states neutral during the war, to sit as a part of the Mixed Arbitral Tribunal in hearing the dispute between Hungary and Roumania.[72] The incident is regarded as important, as it was responsible for the representative of a second great power going on record in favor of holding the requesting of an advisory opinion to be a matter of procedure subject to majority decision.

In 1928 the Swiss delegation placed the following resolution before the Assembly:

The Assembly recommends the Council to consider whether it would not be desirable to submit to the Permanent Court of International Justice, for an advisory opinion the question whether the Council or the Assembly can, by a simple majority, request an advisory opinion under Article 14 of the Covenant of the League of Nations.[73]

It will be remembered that such a suggestion had been made by M. Rolin (Belgium) at the Conference of States Signatories of the Protocol of Signature of the Permanent Court of International Justice in 1926 and that, while it had received considerable support, its adoption had been discouraged by Sir Cecil Hurst (British Empire). The Council discussions in connec-

[71] *Ibid.*, p. 439.
[72] *Ibid.*, p. 446.
[73] *Records of the Ninth Assembly,* Plenary, p. 73.

tion with the "Salamis " case and the dispute between
Hungary and Roumania had since given new life to
the movement to bring about a settlement of this per-
plexing problem. The resolution was submitted by the
Assembly to its First Committee and there received
full consideration. In general, it may be said that in
these debates the members divided into three groups
on this question. One group urged that a speedy solution of the question be sought, expressing at the same
time the belief that the proper solution would be a
recognition that the Council and Assembly can act by
majority vote in requesting advisory opinions. A second small group stated explicitly that an advisory
opinion should be requested only by unanimous vote.
Finally, by far the largest group was of the opinion
that the course followed by the 1926 conference should
again be pursued—that is, no definite commitment on
the subject should be made.

M. Burckhardt (Switzerland) quite naturally defended the Swiss resolution, urging that it was essential
to the well-being of the League to have the point definitely settled.[74] It seems quite clear, also, that he
believed that the answer of the Court would be that a
majority vote of the Assembly or Council should suffice. M. Burckhardt received the active support of
M. Castberg (Norway),[75] M. Rolin (Belgium),[76]
M. Erich (Finland)[77] and M. Limburg (Netherlands)[78]. Two members, M. Politis (Greece) and M.
Djuvara (Roumania) expressed themselves as quite
definitely holding the view that advisory opinions could

[74] *Records of the Ninth Assembly*, First Committee, p. 41.
[75] *Ibid.*, p. 46.
[76] *Ibid.*, p. 47.
[77] *Ibid.*, p. 55.
[78] *Ibid.*, p. 51.

be requested only by unanimous vote. M. Politis stated that " advisory opinions, being in reality no longer such, were accordingly equivalent in the eyes of the Council, of public opinion and of the interested parties to a judgment; and the requirement of unanimity became therefore an inflexible rule." [79] M. Djuvara advanced the arguments that had previously been set forth by M. Titulesco (Roumania) in the Council meetings, adding that the movement to gain advisory opinions by majority vote was an attack upon " the conception which states hold of their sovereignty.[80] While M. Ito (Japan) did not state precisely that he believed advisory opinions should be requested only by unanimous vote, he did state that a decision to request them by majority vote would place such states as Japan, which had not accepted compulsory arbitration, in a very embarrassing position, inasmuch as advisory opinions so closely resemble judgments.[81] Most of the members of the committee, however, followed the leadership of M. Fromageot (France), who declared that the best solution " consisted in giving no answer in advance, but in trusting to the wisdom and to the pacific and equitable spirit of the Council and the Assembly." [82] Sir Cecil Hurst (British Empire) was again present. He suggested as he had in the conference in 1926 that " a short cut was never the best way to reach a perfect result " and that " it would be better to leave it to experience to show what would ultimately constitute the best and most useful rule for the League to follow." [83]

[79] *Ibid.*, p. 46.
[80] *Ibid.*, p. 49.
[81] *Ibid.*, p. 44.
[82] *Ibid.*, p. 40.
[83] *Ibid.*, p. 45.

As a result of these divergencies of opinion the Swiss delegation withdrew its resolution and the committee substituted one which was adopted by the Assembly in the following form:

The Assembly . . . . expresses the desire that, when circumstances permit, the Council may have a study made of the question whether the Council or the Assembly may, by a simple majority, ask for an advisory opinion within the meaning of Article 14 of the Covenant of the League of Nations.[84]

This Assembly resolution was called to the attention of the Council by M. Scialoja (Italy) at a meeting held December 10, 1928. M. Scialoja proposed that each member of the Council should study the problem individually in preparation for an " exchange of views at an early session of the Council." A resolution to this effect was adopted.[85]

The question reappeared in 1930 and on this occasion a small step was taken in the direction of permitting advisory opinions to be requested by majority vote. In accordance with the Assembly resolution of September 24, 1929, the Council appointed at its session of January, 1930, a Commission of Eleven on the " Amendment of the Covenant of the League in order to bring it into harmony with the Pact of Paris." This committee was presided over by M. Scialoja (Italy) and included representatives of Roumania, Germany, British Empire, Spain, Peru, France, Japan, Poland, Sweden, and China.[86] The Committee suggested a number of amendments to the Covenant and included among them was the following which it was proposed to insert in Article 15 immediately following paragraph 7:

At any stage of the examination the Council may, either at the request of one of the parties or on its own initiative, ask the

[84] *Records of the Ninth Assembly,* Plenary, p. 139.
[85] *O. J.,* 1929, p. 10.
[86] *Records of the Eleventh Assembly,* First Committee, p. 104.

Permanent Court of International Justice for an advisory opinion on points of law relating to the dispute. Such application shall not require a unanimous vote by the Council.[87]

The following appears in the report in explanation of this suggested amendment:

The majority of the members of the Committee thought that, in order to render the asking of an advisory opinion easier, the Council should be given the possibility of making a request for an advisory opinion by a decision adopted by a simple majority. The Committee has left entirely on one side the question whether, as a general rule, a request for an advisory opinion requires unanimity or may be made by a simple majority. It has merely intended to make it clear that, in the course of the proceedings of enquiry which take place under Article 15, such opinions would be asked for by a majority decision.[88]

The report of the Committee of Eleven was placed upon the agenda of the Eleventh Assembly and in due course was submitted to the First Committee for its consideration. After debating the proposed amendments long enough to bring out great divergencies in the views held by the members, particularly in regard to the proposed changes relating to sanctions, the First Committee turned the matter over to a sub-committee for further study.[89] This sub-committee reported that " it would be actually in the interests of the success of the proposed amendments that they should be referred to the Governments for further examination." The sub-committee also reported against the insertion of the new paragraph following paragraph 7 of Article 15, stating that " as the obligatory character of the Council's unanimous recommendations has not been retained, it was thought that the principal reason which existed for the insertion of this supplementary provision in

[87] *Ibid.*, p. 109.
[88] *Ibid.*, p. 109.
[89] *Ibid.*, p. 99.

7

the Covenant, and which would have justified its maintenance, no longer existed." [90]

The First Committee, accepting the report of its subcommittee, suggested the following resolution which was adopted by the Eleventh Assembly:

> The Assembly . . . . requests the Secretary-General to submit to the Governments of the Members of the League the report of the Committee of Eleven and that of the First Committee, asking them to formulate their observations before June 1, 1931, and to state, if they so desire, what amendments to the Covenant would, in their opinion, be best suited to attain the object in view.[91]

Quite apart from the question whether the requesting of an advisory opinion is to be regarded as a matter of procedure to be decided by majority vote or a matter of substance to be determined by unanimity, there is the question whether the votes of the parties to the dispute should be reckoned in determining whether the majority vote or the unanimous vote, as the case may be, has in fact been achieved. On at least two occasions, the Council has requested advisory opinions by what has been called a unanimous vote, but was actually a unanimous vote exclusive of the votes of the parties to the dispute. This first occurred in the dispute concerning Eastern Carelia between Russia and Finland,[92] but the Court refused to render the opinion. The Court stated that the submission of a dispute between a non-Member of the League and a Member could take place only by virtue of the consent of the non-Member and that " such consent has never been given by Russia." [93] Thus the Court created a precedent which

[90] *Ibid.,* p. 166.

[91] *Records of the Eleventh Assembly,* Plenary, p. 223.

[92] *O. J.,* 1923, p. 577.

[93] *Permanent Court of International Justice,* Advisory Opinion No. 5, p. 28.

was further strengthened by the Final Act of the Conference of Signatories in 1926, to the effect that requests for advisory opinions will not be entertained in cases in which a non-Member is an actual party unless the non-Member acquiesces.

In the dispute between Turkey and Great Britain over the frontiers of Iraq, submitted to the Council by Great Britain in accordance with the terms of the Treaty of Lausanne and Article 15 of the Covenant, the Council requested an advisory opinion without counting the votes of the parties to the dispute.[94] The step appears to have been taken to overcome the opposition of Turkey to the motion. It should be observed, however, that, while Turkey seemed opposed to the requesting of an advisory opinion, she was cooperating in other respects with the Council in the work of bringing about a peaceful solution of the dispute. The procedure followed by the Council on this occasion appears to have been upheld by the opinion of the Court,[95] and was so interpreted by Sir Cecil Hurst (British Empire) in the Conference of Signatories in 1926.[96] It will be observed, of course, that in this case the Council was working under Article 15, which excludes the votes of the parties to the dispute in the determination of whether unanimity has been achieved.

However, when the Hungarian Optants dispute was before the Council under Article 11 of the Covenant, it was asserted by no less a personage than Lord Robert Cecil that the Council could apply to the Court for an advisory opinion " independently of the parties to the dispute." [97] The line of reasoning followed

[94] *O. J.*, 1925, p. 1377.
[95] *Permanent Court of International Justice,* Advisory Opinion No. 12, p. 32.
[96] See above, p. 73.
[97] *O. J.*, 1923, p. 904.

by Cecil in arriving at this interesting conclusion will
be dealt with below in connection with a more detailed
consideration of the practice that has been established
by the League in regard to when the votes of parties to
the dispute are counted and when excluded.[98]

It is the opinion of the writer that a majority vote
by the Assembly or by the Council should be sufficient
for requesting an advisory opinion from the World
Court and, furthermore, that such a practice will ultimately be established. It will be remembered that Article 5, paragraph 2, of the Covenant has been interpreted in such a fashion as to permit the Council and
the Assembly to set up as well as to appoint the members of committees of inquiry to establish facts and
committees of jurists to give legal advice. It has always
been understood that such bodies are purely advisory,
the Assembly and Council being in no way obligated
to accept the advice tendered. To hold unanimity essential for the creation of such bodies would have seriously
impaired the efficient functioning of League organs,
particularly in the settling of disputes. Now when the
World Court renders an advisory opinion on a legal
question, it is fulfilling exactly the same function as a
committee of jurists specially set up by a majority vote
of the Assembly or Council. To be sure, the Council
or Assembly is more inclined to act upon such legal
advice from the Court because of the prestige of that
body than they would upon the same advice coming
from a committee of jurists. Nevertheless, there is no
legal obligation compelling acceptance of the advice
tendered, such as there is in cases in which the Court
renders a judgment. Indeed, it seems probable that the
Assembly or Council might quite conceivably decide

[98] See below, p. 134 ff.

to disregard an advisory opinion should it be offered by a very small majority of the Court.

Perhaps the greatest obstacle in the way of the general acceptance of this view is that in actual practice some disputes of a purely legal character are submitted to the Council for settlement instead of being submitted to the Court. In such cases, when the Council asks for an advisory opinion on the legal points involved, it is in fact asking for an opinion on the substance of the dispute rather than upon questions which are merely preliminary to a solution of the larger questions at issue. However, as the prestige of the Court increases and as the number of states adhering to the optional clause of the World Court Statute becomes greater, this situation will change. Disputes of a purely legal nature will be referred directly to the Court for adjudication, the Council and Assembly confining themselves to the consideration of disputes of a political character. In cases of the latter type, the legal issues which arise will be truly preliminary questions which must be cleared away before the main issues can be dealt with. It would then no longer seem dangerous to refer to the Court for advisory opinions, for it would not mean that in effect, the Council or Assembly was passing its jurisdiction over to another body. The Council or Assembly, as the case might be, would still retain control, merely having the benefit of the best legal advice in clearing the ground for a consideration of the main political issues involved. The application for an advisory opinion would then be viewed as a truly procedural step, a step taken by way of preparation for a consideration of the substantive questions involved. It is hardly conceivable that, when the request for advisory opinions has been confined to questions of this character, the League will tolerate such obstructions as could be brought about by the unanimity rule. It will consider the consequences and see to it that the machinery necessary to settle a dispute can be applied without a single member or small group of members having it in their power effectively to obstruct action.

That this development has been anticipated by many of the most influential members of the Assembly and the Council seems apparent. Such men as Sir Cecil Hurst and M. Fromageot appear to have perceived the danger of attempting to force the League to go on record immediately in favor of permitting the Council or Assembly to request advisory opinions by majority vote at a time when the distinction that should exist between disputes of a legal and of a political character is not properly observed. Such a course would no doubt be politically inexpedient. However, they have been equally alive to the importance of holding open the question of the vote necessary to request advisory opinions even at a moment when great advantage might have come from a definite commitment to unanimity. But when the practice is established of submitting all those disputes of a strictly legal character to the World Court or to some arbitral tribunal, the Council and Assembly being resorted to only in disputes of a political nature, the League may be expected to decide that advisory opinions may be requested by majority vote.

CHAPTER IV

MODIFICATIONS OF UNANIMITY ACHIEVED THROUGH
PRACTICE (*Continued*)

"DECISIONS" AND "RECOMMENDATIONS"

The first paragraph of Article 5 of the Covenant provides that " decisions " at any meeting of the Assembly or Council shall be taken by unanimous vote unless the Covenant or treaties specifically provide to the contrary; and the second paragraph, as we have seen, provides that exception shall be made for matters of procedure. At first glance one would, no doubt, conclude that the article required all resolutions not pertaining to matters of procedure or to other matters specifically exempted from the general rule to be passed by unanimous vote. However, such is not the case in the Assembly, for that body has held that the word " decision " refers to a resolution in which it is the intention to impose a definite legal obligation. Where it is only the intention of the Assembly to suggest, advise or recommend a certain line of conduct, a " decision " is not taken and hence the Covenant is not interpreted as requiring unanimity. That this interpretation of the word " decision " is of far reaching importance in minimizing the rigors of the unanimity requirement in the Assembly will be readily apparent.

The " recommendation " as a means by which the Assembly could escape the necessity of achieving unanimity was first resorted to in the First Assembly, the initial use occurring in connection with the selection of the non-permanent members of the Council, a matter which has been referred to above in connection with the question of what constitutes matters of procedure. It will be recalled that the First Committee had suggested a series of five resolutions to the Assembly and that the committee *rapporteur*, Mr. Balfour (British Empire) stated that none of these resolutions had been passed by unanimous vote in the committee. When it became apparent that the resolutions as reported by the committee could not receive unanimous approval in the plenary meeting, Balfour proposed the deletion of some and changes in others. In regard to the fourth resolution which provided for selection of the non-permanent members of the Council on a regional basis, Balfour suggested the substitution of a recommendation. He worded this recommendation as follows:

> The Assembly is recommended to vote for the four non-permanent Members of the Council to be selected by the Assembly in 1920 so that three shall be selected from among the Members of the League in Europe and the two American Continents, and one selected from the Members in Asia and the remaining parts of the world.[1]

In explanation Balfour said:

> You will observe that I have substantially taken the fourth paragraph of the committee's report and have turned it, not into a substantive proposal which runs counter or may be thought to run counter to the Covenant, but into a recommendation to the members of the Assembly to cast their votes next week in a particular way.[2]

The President, M. Hymans (Belgium), in summing up Balfour's proposals described this one as " a *voeu,* which in English is known as a recommendation." [3] The recommendation was carried by a vote of 27 for to 4 votes against.[4] In accordance with the terms of the recommendation, the Assembly selected Belgium, Bra-

---

[1] *Records of the First Assembly,* Plenary, p. 433.
[2] *Ibid.,* p. 433.
[3] *Ibid.,* p. 434.
[4] *Ibid.,* p. 435.

zil, Spain and China to occupy the non-permanent Council seats.

On another occasion during the meetings of the First Assembly, President Hymans (Belgium) resorted to similar tactics in order to prevent the defeat of a resolution. The Sixth Committee had submitted a resolution on armaments to the Assembly, paragraph " e " of which was as follows:

Pending the full execution of the measures for the reduction of armaments recommended by Article 8 of the Covenant, the Committee invites the Assembly to request the Council to submit for the consideration of the Members of the League the acceptance of an undertaking not to exceed for the first two financial years following the next financial year, the sum total of expenditure on the military, naval and air services provided for in the latter Budget subject, however, to account being taken of the following reservations:

1. Any contributions of troops, war material and money recommended by the League of Nations, with a view to the fulfillment of obligations imposed by Article 16 of the Covenant or by the Treaties registered by the League.

2. Exceptional conditions notified as such to the Council of the League of Nations in accordance with the spirit of paragraphs 2 and 6 of Article 8 of the Covenant.[5]

Mr. G. N. Barnes (British Empire), supported by many other delegates, spoke in favor of the resolutions, pointing out that paragraph " e " provided for making a real start in the limitation of armaments.[6] M. Leon Bourgeois (France), however, taking the position that France has continually occupied ever since the war, declared budgetary limitation to be manifestly unfair and announced his opposition to it.[7] Mr. Fisher (British Empire), scenting the danger of having the entire resolution defeated because France opposed budgetary limitation, suggested that paragraph " e " be separated

[5] *Ibid.*, p. 508.
[6] *Ibid.*, p. 511.
[7] *Ibid.*, p. 512.

from the other portions of the resolution so that the Assembly could vote upon it separately.[8] The President, M. Hymans (Belgium), thereupon made the following suggestion concerning the much contested paragraph:

> If we leave this paragraph as it stands with its present wording and context, it will require a unanimous vote. I therefore propose to the Assembly that we should simply turn this paragraph into a recommendation. If we read it carefully, we shall see that it is nothing but a recommendation.
>
> I suggest, therefore, to the Assembly that we should alter its form and say: " The Assembly recommends to the Council to submit for the consideration of the Governments . . . ."
>
> If the Assembly accepts this suggestion, a unanimous decision will no longer be necessary; we should simply have to vote on the recommendation, for which only a majority is required.[9]

That the members of the Assembly did not at the time understand clearly the distinction that was being drawn for them between " decisions " and "recommendations " is shown by the following statement made by Mr. Barnes (British Empire) :

> I am not quite clear as to the full meaning of your suggested amendment, Mr. President, but if it has the effect of weakening this resolution, I hope that the Assembly will stick to the resolution as it stands. It seems to me that this is the only operative part of the Report now before us. We have, after a good many words, a definite proposal. It is only a proposal that the Council should request the Governments to do something. That is all. The Governments, as has been pointed out by Mr. Fisher, are not obliged to do it. They are simply asked by the Council to do it. That to my mind is weak enough. If the object of your suggestion is to weaken further this proposal, I can only say that I for my part, very much regret it.[10]

To this the President replied:

> In my opinion when one reads the text carefully, one sees that in reality we are dealing only with a recommendation. I propose to

---

[8] *Ibid.,* p. 527.
[9] *Ibid.,* p. 529.
[10] *Ibid.,* p. 530.

give it officially the form of a recommendation in order that it may have an appropriate title. We shall then be able to vote it by simple majority.[11]

M. Hymans thus appears to be of the opinion that whenever there is no intention to bind the Governments to a particular line of conduct the Assembly may act by majority vote.

Lord Robert Cecil (South Africa) then suggested that paragraph " e " should first be put to a vote as a resolution and then if it should fail to achieve unanimity it should be voted as a recommendation.[12] He also made a spirited appeal to those states who found themselves opposed to the resolution to abstain from voting so unanimity might be obtained. He spoke in part as follows:

Now, in this Report the one definite proposal towards general disarmament is contained in this paragraph " e." I had hoped, I confess, when I heard the speech of M. Bourgeois, that though he was not able, on behalf of the French delegation, to vote for this paragraph, he would not find it absolutely necessary to vote against it. I thought he was going to abstain, and we could then have had the advantage of carrying this as a resolution. But I confess I feel, myself, great reluctance in assenting to anything which will in fact weaken or water down this resolution, and when the President asks us, in a very persuasive manner, to agree to this proposal, I feel, if we agree to it, it would be making all the members of the Assembly say we lowered this from a resolution into a mere pious expression of hope. I confess I think that is asking a very great step from the Assembly. If there are members of the Assembly who either by their instruction, or for other reasons, feel themselves bound to vote against this resolution, they must take the responsibility before the world, but I venture to appeal to my colleagues not to take that extreme course, and in that way they will free their Governments from any responsibility, if responsibility can attach to us, and at the same time allow the Assembly to do what I am perfectly

[11] *Ibid.*, p. 530.
[12] *Ibid.*, p. 531.

certain the vast majority of the Assembly desires to do, namely, to place this resolution on record as a first step towards the disarmament which they desire to be taken.[13]

When the vote was taken on the resolution, the words " the Assembly recommends to the Council " being substituted for " the Assembly requests the Council," [14] thirty voted for, seven against, [15] and one abstained.[16] Thus the resolution failed to achieve unanimity but it was announced as passing in the form of a recommendation.[17] The Council, in accordance with the terms of the recommendation, submitted for the consideration of the Governments the plan for budgetary limitation of armaments.

In the first year of the League's existence, the Colombian delegation, disturbed by the "danger that the negative vote of some delegation may prevent the realization of the lofty ideals which inspired the Articles of the Covenant," [18] suggested the following amendment to Article 5 of the Covenant to be inserted immediately following paragraph 1:

This procedure [unanimity] shall not apply to decisions of the Assembly which aim at the development in practice of the provisions or principles laid down in this Covenant. In such cases a two-thirds majority of the Members of the League represented at the Assembly shall suffice.[19]

---

[13] *Ibid.*, p. 532.

[14] The French text was changed from " la Commission invite l'Assemblée à prier le Conseil " to " l'Assemblée emet le voeu que le Conseil."

[15] Brazil, Chile, France, Greece, Poland, Roumania, Uruguay.

[16] Siam.

[17] *Records of the First Assembly,* Plenary, p. 535.

[18] *Ibid.*, p. 257.

[19] *Committee on Amendments to the Covenant:* First Report to the Council, p. 12. (League Doc. A. 24. 1921. V.)

This proposed amendment, together with all others suggested during the first year of the League, was submitted by the Council to the Committee on Amendments to the Covenant (usually referred to as the London Committee) for study. The report of this Committee was submitted at the direction of the Council to the Second Assembly,where it was considered by the First Committee of that body. In both the Committee on Amendments and the First Committee of the Second Assembly, the Colombian amendment stimulated interesting debate on the nature of "decisions" and "recommendations."

The London Committee reported against the Colombian amendment. It felt that the distinction which the authors of the amendment sought to draw between decisions which did and those which did not "aim at the development in practice of the provisions laid down in the Covenant" could not be made sufficiently clear for it to serve as the basis for an exception to the rule of unanimity. Moreover, the Committee found additional departures from unanimity in the Assembly to be unnecessary. They observed that Assembly resolutions were of two kinds—"decisions" and "recommendations." In the case of "decisions" the committee was of the opinion that "the unanimity rule, which protects the sovereignty of states, ought to be maintained." On the other hand, "in accordance with the practice which has already been adopted by the First Assembly, and which deserves to be encouraged and developed," the committee was of the opinion that all resolutions of the nature of recommendations might be passed by a simple majority vote. The Committee further pointed out that, "in accordance with Article 5, the only resolutions which require unanimity are decisions, properly so-called, which are capable of definitely binding States Members, and not simple recommendations." [20] The First Committee of the Second Assembly shared the view held by the London Committee that the Colombian amendment was unnecessary, at least, in the form in which it was submitted. The committees were also in essential agreement on the question of when unanimity was required in the Assembly. The First Committee expressed its agreement with the statement in the London Committee's report to the effect that unanimity serves to safeguard the sovereignty of states. From this they deduced that unanimity could not be necessary except in cases in which the sovereignty of states was in jeopardy. Hence, a majority vote suffices for addressing recommendations or requests to the Council or to the member states. Moreover, they held it to be " an irrefutable fact " that many of the resolutions voted by the First Assembly could in no way be distinguished from recommendations and might have been adopted by a majority vote.[21]

Inasmuch as the Assembly practice of holding that those resolutions which impose no immediate legal obligation upon the member states may be passed in the form of recommendations requiring only majority vote had thus been sanctioned by the Committee on Amendments to the Covenant appointed by the Council and by the Assembly's own First Committee, that body felt free to continue the practice. Consequently, numerous rulings have since been made on what may properly be considered a resolution embodying a recommendation to be voted by majority and what is to be considered as a decision requiring unanimity.

[20] *Ibid.*, p. 12.
[21] *Records of the Second Assembly*, First Committee, p. 179.

It has been the practice of the Assembly to hold that constitutional resolutions, that is, those which give an interpretation to the provisions of the Covenant, are decisions requiring unanimous vote. A ruling to this effect was first made in the Second Assembly and the precedent created was strengthened by the Fourth Assembly. The formation of the precedent came about as a result of an amendment to Article 18 of the Covenant being submitted by the First Committee to the Assembly for consideration. When it became apparent that there was no approach to agreement upon the proposed amendment in the Assembly, Mr. Balfour (British Empire) moved the adoption of the following resolution:

The Assembly, taking note of the proposal for the amendment of Article 18 contained in the report of Committee number 1 decides to adjourn further consideration until the Third Assembly, it being understood that, in the meantime, Members of the League are at liberty to interpret their obligations under Article 18 in conformity with the proposed amendment.[22]

M. Restrepo (Colombia) requested that the resolution be divided into two parts, one providing for adjourning consideration until the Third Assembly and the other providing that the Members are at liberty to interpret Article 18 in conformity with the proposed amendment.[23] When the second resolution was put to the vote, however, the result was announced as 28 for and 5 against.[24] The President, M. Van Karnebeek (Netherlands), believing this resolution to be a recommendation, announced its passage.[25] However, at the next plenary meeting, after M. Restrepo (Colombia)

[22] *Records of the Second Assembly*, Plenary, p. 851.
[23] *Ibid.*, p. 852.
[24] *Ibid.*, p. 852.
[25] *Ibid.*, p. 852.

had raised the point of order, the President reversed his holding, explaining the situation as follows:

> You will remember that, according to the voting, 28 were in favor and 5 against. If we were concerned with a resolution [*d'une resolution*], this would have meant its rejection. On the other hand, if we were dealing with a suggestion [*d'une suggestion*] or recommendation [*d'un voeu*] it would have meant adoption.
>
> I must admit that at the outset I was of the opinion that the motion in question was a recommendation, but I must confess to you that, after this morning's meetings, I have carefully considered the text which was submitted to you, and upon which you voted, and I am now of the opinion that what we had before us was a resolution.
>
> The second part is governed, in my opinion, by the word decides [*décide*] which occurs in the first part. Moreover, I have the impression that we are dealing with an interpretative decision [*d'une decision interprétative*].[26]

M. Scialoja (Italy) thereupon spoke as follows:

> I maintained this morning that the second part of Mr. Balfour's proposal was of a nature to constitute a wider interpretation of Article 18. The vote showed that a large majority of the members of this Assembly favored this view, and that only a small minority was opposed. We have here a decision of the Assembly, and I think that the President is perfectly right in maintaining that in the case of a resolution unanimity is necessary.
>
> Unanimity is required for an affirmative decision, so that we can not say that the resolution was approved by the Assembly. Neither can we say, however, that it was rejected. We can merely say that it was not accepted. If we say that it was rejected, the opposite interpretation becomes involved, and it might be thought that the interpretation adopted was contrary to the interpretation proposed, which would be the exact opposite of the Assembly's intention. We must, therefore, say that the proposal was not accepted, which I think will meet the case.[27]

The President summed up the situation by stating that all were in agreement with M. Scialoja.[28]

[26] *Ibid.*, p. 895.
[27] *Ibid.*, p. 895.
[28] *Ibid.*, p. 895.

That the ruling made by President Van Karnebeek (Netherlands) in the Second Assembly and interpreted by M. Scialoja (Italy) has actually established a precedent subsequently followed by the later Assemblies was made evident by the famous case of the Assembly's attempts to define the scope of the obligations contained in Article 10 of the Covenant. The vote on the interpretive resolution in the Fourth Assembly was 29 for the resolution, one against,[29] and 22 absent or abstaining.[30] The President, M. de la Torriente y Peraza (Cuba) after announcing the result of the vote said:

A resolution containing an interpretation of an article in the Covenant can only be adopted by a unanimous vote.

As unanimity has not been obtained, I am unable to declare the proposed resolution adopted.

In accordance, however, with a precedent which arose in a similar case, I shall not declare the motion rejected, because it cannot be argued that, in voting as it has done, the Assembly has pronounced in favor of the converse interpretation.

I accordingly declare the proposal not adopted.

It may nevertheless be advisable that the result of the voting and names of the members who voted should be communicated to the Council, which may regard the result as important.

I propose, then, that the result of the voting on the draft resolution should be communicated to the Council.[31]

Assembly practice has also decreed that, when that body states in a resolution that it " is of the opinion," a unanimous vote is necessary. Such a precedent was established by the Second Assembly during its consideration of the allocation of League expenses. The

[29] Persia.

[30] For a list of the absent or abstaining states, see *Records of the Fourth Assembly,* Plenary, p. 87. Of the 22, nine were actually absent. The absent or abstaining included no powers having permanent Council seats.

[31] *Records of the Fourth Assembly,* Plenary, p. 87.

8

following resolution was submitted by the Fourth Committee to the plenary session:

> The Assembly is of the opinion that when a revised scheme of allocation of the expenses of the League has been adopted after consideration of the fresh recommendations of the Expert Committee, it would be equitable that Members of the League which may, with effect from January 1, 1921, and up to the year for which the revised scheme is adopted, have paid more than they are called upon to pay under the operation of such a scheme, should be entitled to the refund of the excess amount paid.[32]

The following rather amusing discussion took place concerning this resolution:

M. Urrutia (Colombia): " Before the vote is taken, I ask for an explanation on the point whether the resolution before us is of a character that must be adopted unanimously or by a three-fourths majority. I understand that the three-fourths majority is necessary for the adoption of amendments, but that for resolutions which are not submitted to the approval of governments unanimity is necessary." [33]

The President, Mr. Van Karnebeek (Netherlands): " I agree with the delegate of Colombia that when we are dealing with a resolution unanimity is necessary; but the question before us is precisely whether we are dealing with a resolution or only a recommendation; that is to say, with a statement of an opinion. I do not know what is the opinion of the *rapporteur,* but personally I think that, in the case of this additional resolution, we are dealing with a simple recommendation; that is to say, with the expression of a desire and of an opinion."

M. Aguero (Cuba): " No, it is a resolution."

The President: " If the *rapporteur* thinks that it is a resolution I will put it to the vote.

[32] *Records of the Second Assembly,* Plenary, p. 886.
[33] *Ibid.,* p. 887.

"The chairman and *rapporteur* of the Committee have informed me that we have before us a recommendation. I accept the view of these gentlemen, who are best qualified to decide this point . . . ."

M. Fernandes (Brazil) : "To whom is the recommendation addressed?"

M. Hanotaux (France) : "It is a recommendation which involves making payments."

M. Hymans (Belgium) : "To whom is the recommendation addressed?"

The President: "To all the members of the League. We have often had to vote on recommendations drafted in this rather vague way. As the Chairman and the *rapporteur* of the Committee are of opinion that this is a recommendation. . . . ."

M. Hymans: "To whom?"

The President: "In order to clear up this question it would, perhaps, be better to alter the wording of the proposal. I repeat, gentlemen, that the Chairman and *rapporteur* of the committee, who have been asked to give the Committee's opinion, submit to you the proposal in the form of a recommendation."

M. Hanotaux (France) : "As an obligation will be created, the proposal cannot be considered as a simple recommendation."

The President: "Committee no. 4 proposes to substitute the word ' recommends ' [*recommende*] for the words ' is of the opinion that ' [*estime*]."

The recommendation was thereupon adopted by a vote of twenty-one for to ten against.[34]

The Assembly can express a wish by majority vote even when the wish is that Members of the League adopt without delay the conventions embodied in the final act

[34] *Ibid.*, p. 888.

of a conference. When this ruling was made, M. Hanotaux (France) objected, asserting that a majority vote
was not sufficient where the signing of a convention
was involved. The President, however, overruled him,
holding that the resolution was beyond doubt one which
expressed " a wish and a recommendation." [35]

The situation in regard to Assembly resolutions
might be summed up by stating that, in general, it has
been the practice of that body to hold that unanimity
is essential whenever the resolution under consideration is of such a character as to impose a legal obligation upon the member states or whenever it is one
which purports to interpret the Covenant or to give
an authoritative expression of the view held by the
Assembly on any question. However, resolutions in
which the Assembly recommends or expresses a wish or
a hope may be adopted by majority vote. Obviously,
these have no legal force but they do possess a moral
force, the extent of which depends in large part, of
course, upon how nearly unanimity has been
approached and upon the importance of the states constituting the minority.

As might be expected, the recommendation is frequently resorted to when unanimity can not be
achieved. In those Assembly resolutions which con-
tain recommendations to the Council or to the Member
States, as a large proportion of the Assembly resolutions do, the adjustment can be easily made. A few
examples from Assembly practice, in addition to those
already given, will make this clear.

In the Tenth Assembly a resolution was introduced
calling for endorsement of a resolution adopted by the
Conference for Revision of the Statute of the Permanent Court to the effect that candidates nominated for

[35] *Ibid.*, p. 528.

the position of judge by the national groups should possess recognized experience in international law and should be able to read both official languages of the court and speak at least one of them. This was passed in the form of a recommendation, thirty-two voting for, fifteen against, and one abstaining.[36]

In the Fourth Assembly, as in the First, a recommendation was adopted in respect to regional representation being observed in the selection of the nonpermanent Members of the Council. On this occasion M. Motta (Switzerland) observed that this recommendation lacked legal force but had great moral force.[37] A similar recommendation had been passed in the Third Assembly.[38]

In the Second Assembly a resolution calling upon states to ratify the conventions embodied in the Final Act of the Conference of Geneva on the Traffic in Women and Children was changed into a recommendation to the Governments to take this action. The change was made owing to opposition on the part of the representatives of France, supported by the representatives of several of the small powers. The recommendation was adopted by thirty votes for, none against, and twenty-one, including France, abstaining.[39]

Recommendations voted by a large majority of the Assembly including the votes of all the great powers no doubt have substantially the same weight with the Council and with the Member States as those recommendations which have achieved absolute unanimity. On the other hand, those voted by small majorities or by majorities made up of the smaller states can not

[36] *Records of the Tenth Assembly,* Plenary, p. 121.
[37] *Records of the Fourth Assembly,* Plenary, p. 114.
[38] *Records of the Third Assembly,* Plenary, p. 350.
[39] *Records of the Second Assembly,* Plenary, p. 528.

be expected to command much respect. In the latter case it seems probable that Assembly recommendations would be ignored, thus giving rise to a situation which would cause a diminishing of Assembly prestige. This danger was appreciated by a sub-committee of the First Committee of the Second Assembly. After they had considered the amendment to Article 5 proposed by the Colombian delegation and had decided against it, they suggested on their own initiative the insertion of the following paragraph immediately following the first paragraph of the Article:

Any resolution of the Assembly which amounted not to an individual engagement by each Member of the League but to a request or a recommendation addressed either to the Council or to all the Members of the League, might be adopted with only a two-thirds majority of the members represented at the meeting.[40]

Thus the committee, feeling that the Colombian distinction between resolutions which " aim at the development in practice of the provisions laid down in the Covenant " and those which involve new commitments was unsound, discarded it and substituted this proposed amendment by which it was intended to prevent the passage of recommendations by simple majorities, with a consequent diminishing of Assembly prestige. This proposed amendment was never given serious consideration by the Assembly.

It does not appear that the power to adopt recommendations by a simple majority vote has been abused. In only a few cases have they been passed by a bare majority, and there has been no case in which all or even most of the great powers have found themselves in the minority. On the other hand, the device has great value in that it allows the Assembly to recommend a course of action either to the Council or to the

[40] *Records of the Second Assembly,* First Committee, p. 179.

member states in spite of vociferous objection by states which may have selfish interests to protect.

The Council has never in its practice drawn the distinction between " decisions " and " recommendations " which has been adopted by the Assembly, although by the same line of reasoning employed by the Assembly it might do so. It would seem that the " decisions " mentioned in Article 5 of the Covenant should logically have the same meaning for the Council as for the Assembly. However, the Committee on Amendments to the Covenant, which sanctioned the adoption of recommendations by a majority vote of the Assembly, went definitely on record as opposed to the practice in the Council. It was their opinion that all resolutions, whether decisions properly so-called, or simple recommendations, should be adopted unanimously by the Council. They justified this difference in practice between the two bodies by observing that the Council is the " essentially active organ of the League, and above all performs duties of an executive nature." In order to accomplish this task, the Council should be possessed of great authority and that authority is definitely enhanced by the knowledge that all of its actions rest upon unanimous agreement. They also pointed out that inasmuch as the Council is much smaller than the Assembly unanimity would be much easier to attain.[41]

The First Committee of the Second Assembly announced itself as in complete agreement with this view expressed by the London Committee. They saw no reason for extending the Assembly practice of voting recommendations by majority to the Council, for that body, because of its small size, may prolong dis-

[41] *Committee on Amendments to the Covenant:* First Report to the Council, p. 12. (League Doc. A. 24. 1921. V.)

cussion until agreement is reached. Moreover, they pointed out that "two years' experience has shown that unanimity does not in any way hinder the Council's activity, but that it is rather a guarantee of continued agreement between its Members, which is essential for the authority of their decisions." [42]

Two questions might be raised concerning the validity of the conclusions reached by these committees. First, has the experience of ten additional years, with an enlarged Council, borne out the conclusion of the two committees that the Council is not hindered by the unanimity rule? Secondly, how can the conclusion of the London Committee, endorsed by the Assembly committee, to the effect that Council authority depends on the maintenance of unanimity, be reconciled with the many explicit provisions in numerous international instruments authorizing Council action by a majority?

The significance of these interpretations in respect to "decisions" and "recommendations" will be discussed again in connection with the Assembly and Article 19 of the Covenant and also in relation to the application of certain articles by the Council. [43]

"DECISIONS" AND "RESOLUTIONS OF AMENDMENT"

Another exception of great importance to the general rule of unanimity has been brought about by the interpretation placed upon the word "decisions" of Article 5 in relation to Article 26 of the Covenant. Article 26 reads as follows:

Amendments to this Covenant will take effect when ratified by the Members of the League whose representatives compose the Council and by a majority of the Members of the League whose representatives compose the Assembly.

---

[42] *Records of the Second Assembly,* First Committee, p. 177.
[43] See below, pp. 154-157.

No such amendment shall bind any member of the League which signifies its dissent therefrom, but in that case it shall cease to be a Member of the League.

It will be observed that the article is silent on the question of how amendments shall be proposed, specifying only that they will take effect when ratified by Members of the League whose representatives compose the Council and by a majority of the Members of the League whose representatives compose the Assembly. Since no specific exception is made from the general rule of unanimity prescribed for both Council and Assembly in Article 5, it would seem that, in strict accordance with the words of the Covenant, unanimity should be required for the proposal of amendments. Indeed, several publicists of acknowledeged standing immediately sprang to this conclusion and, in spite of the Assembly's decision to the contrary, the mistaken belief that unanimity is required for the proposal of amendments still persists to a considerable extent.[44]

The problem of determining the vote necessary for the proposal of amendments, as distinct from ratification, was first given formal attention by the League in its second year. The question was referred to the First Committee of the Second Assembly for study. That body, by a vote of twenty-one to four, expressed the belief that for the proposal of amendments a majority vote, including the votes of all members having representation on the Council, should suffice.[45] The line of reasoning followed by the majority of the committee in arriving at this conclusion seems significant as an

[44] See, for instance, C. Van Vollenhoven's introduction to C. A. Kluyver, *Documents on the League of Nations*, p. 9, and Philip Baker in Rask-Orstedfonden, *Les Origines et l'Oeuvre de la Société des Nations*, II, 66.

[45] *Records of the Second Assembly*, First Committee, p. 65.

indication of the attitude assumed toward the unanimity requirement as such.[46] First of all, it was asserted that, if unanimity was insisted upon for the proposal of amendments " through a narrow, legal interpretation of Article 26," it would be virtually impossible to amend the Covenant, and, as a result of this, the arrangements made in Paris in 1919 would have to be looked upon as permanent and unchangeable.[47] Secondly, it was asserted that unanimity should be applied only to carry out the · principle which inspired it, namely, the protection of the sovereignty of states. Inasmuch as the second paragraph of Article 26 specifically provided for the right of secession for those unwilling to be bound by an amendment, they asserted that sovereignty was adequately safeguarded. In the third place, it was contended that resolutions proposing amendments to the Covenant are in no sense decisions within the meaning of Article 5, since they entirely lack binding force until coming into effect as amendments after having received ratification by a certain number of states as provided in Article 26. This, it will be observed, is the same argument that had been so successfully used in justifying the adoption of recommendations by a majority vote of the Assembly. In

[46] See *Records of the Second Assembly*, First Committee, pp. 43-68 and 177-180; also *Records of the Second Assembly*, Plenary, pp. 676-681; 708-711; 723-735

[47] See especially the remarks of Mr. Balfour (British Empire) *Records of the Second Assembly*, First Committee, p. 50. See also the remark of M. Seferiades (Greece) in the *Second Assembly*, Plenary, p. 681, where he likened a League with a unanimity requirement for proposing amendments to " a prison with the smallest minority for its jailer, a prison with thick and impassable walls, with a Sleeping Beauty in its keep, lying amidst an untold wealth of dreams and aspirations, but incapable of awakening or acting for the good of the community."

the fourth place, it was stated that the authors of the Covenant had intended to provide for the proposal of amendments by majority vote. To substantiate this contention there was quoted that part of Wilson's speech made at the Peace Conference, April 28, 1919, in which he stated that Article 26 makes possible the amendment of the Covenant by a majority of the states composing the Assembly instead of a three-fourths vote as previously required, although retaining unanimity for the Council. The three members of the First Committee who had been members of the Paris Commission were all of the opinion that it was the intention of the Commission that a majority should suffice.[48] In the fifth place, it was alleged that, at the time of the ratification of the Covenant by the various Governments, it had been in several cases pointed out that amendments to the Covenant could be proposed by a majority vote of the Assembly, including the votes of all those states having Council seats. This contention was bolstered by documentary evidence.[49] Finally, it was asserted that if a reasonable, common-sense interpretation was to be given to Article 26, a majority vote would have to be held sufficient for proposing amendments, for it would be quite absurd to interpret it as meaning that unanimity is required for proposal and only a majority for ratification.

The assault on these arguments, which were advanced by the majority of the committee, was led by Professor Demetre Negulesco (Roumania) and Professor A. A. H. Struycken (Netherlands) supported by M. Manini Rios (Uruguay), M. Sastri (India),

[48] They were .M. Scialoja (Italy), Mr. Wellington Koo (China) and M. Hymans (Belgium). See also the remarks of M. Rolin (Belgium), *Records of the Second Assembly*, First Committee, p. 54.

[49] *Records of the Second Assembly*, First Committee, p. 159.

M. Palacios (Spain), M. Freire d'Andrade (Portugal), and M. Osusky (Czechoslovakia). Quite naturally no state possessing a permanent Council seat was interested in insisting upon absolute unanimity for the proposal of amendments. They were adequately protected by the provision that the majority should include the votes of all states having Council representation. Moreover, the minority included only the representative of one state, Spain, which occupied at the time a temporary Council seat.

M. Negulesco (Roumania) launched the attack upon the majority position by calling to the attention of the committee the stipulation in Article 5 that " except where otherwise expressly provided in this Covenant " unanimity was essential. Admittedly Article 26 did not specify majority decisions for the proposal of amendments. Therefore, to allow them to be proposed in that fashion would be to violate the terms of the Covenant. Moreover, M. Negulesco was able to supply a plausible motive for the wording of Article 26 by the drafters of the Covenant. Experience had shown, he said, that states were very slow to ratify conventions even after their signatures had been given. Hence, it was the intention of the authors of the Covenant to retain the unanimity requirement for the first and easier part of the procedure, namely, for proposal, and to waive unanimity for the more difficult part— ratification.[50]

M. Struycken (Netherlands) stated that in his opinion there were only two possible positions to take on this question. In the first place, one might consider the vote of the Assembly as an essential factor in the procedure of revising the Covenant, in which case no

[50] *Ibid.*, p. 44.

exception from unanimity having been made in Article 26, a unanimous vote would be necessary. Or, instead, one might hold that, since Article 26 speaks only of ratification, the initiative in proposing changes should come from outside the League, that is, from the signatory states themselves. Here again unanimity would be essential. Furthermore, M. Struycken stated that it was unreasonable to interpret the amending clause in a manner that allowed amendments to the fundamental law of the League to be proposed by a smaller vote than was required for the proposal of ordinary conventions. This would clearly be in conflict with the procedure followed in all states having written constitutions.[51] The majority group in the committee answered this charge with the assertion that an amendment is merely the perfecting of an agreement already entered into by unanimous consent while a draft convention embodies the plan for an entirely new agreement.

The majority statement to the effect that sovereignty was adequately protected by the right that each state possessed of withdrawing from the League was answered by M. Struycken by calling attention to the obvious truth that in most cases a state which opposed an amendment would be unable to protect itself by withdrawing from the League. It would have to balance its interests and decide whether it would have more to gain by withdrawing or by remaining. As the League assumes direction of more functions and as it approaches universality, withdrawal will become an almost impossible choice.[52] In answer to the majority statement that it was the intention of the authors of

51 *Ibid.*, p. 48.
52 *Ibid.*, p. 48.

the Covenant, as shown by the speech of President Wilson, that amendments be proposed by a majority of the Assembly including the votes of all members having at the time Council seats, M. Struycken simply stated that no weight could be attached to such arguments since the statements of Wilson had been uttered subsequent to the drafting of Articles 5 and 26.[53]

In order to facilitate an agreement, M. Rolin (Belgium) submitted the following proposal:

With a view to meeting henceforward the objections expressed by certain delegates with regard to the procedure enabling amendments to be carried by a majority vote of the Assembly, the committee decides to recommend that the Assembly should accept no amendment at that session unless it receives a three-fourths majority.[54]

The committee likewise proposed that Article 26 of the Covenant be amended to read as follows:

Amendments to the present Covenant the text of which shall have been voted by the Assembly on a three-fourths majority, in which there shall be included the votes of all the Members of the Council represented at the meeting, will take effect when ratified by the Members of the League whose representatives composed the Council when the vote was taken, and by the majority of those whose representatives form the Assembly.

If the required number of ratifications shall not have been obtained within twenty-two months after the vote of the Assembly, the proposed amendment shall remain without effect.

The Secretary-General shall inform the Members of the taking effect of the amendment.

Any member of the League which has not at that time ratified the amendment is free to notify the Secretary-General within a year of its refusal to accept it, but in that case it shall cease to be a Member of the League.[55]

These amendments to Article 26, in the form here given, and the recommendation that at the present ses-

[53] *Ibid.*, p. 48.
[54] *Ibid.*, p. 63.
[55] *Records of the Second Assembly*, Plenary, p. 733.

sion no amendments be passed without a three-fourths majority, in slightly changed form, were put to a vote in the Assembly. The President, M. Van Karnebeek (Netherlands) announced in each case that a majority vote would suffice for adoption. The recommendation and each of the resolutions proposing amendments passed by a vote of thirty-seven for, none against, and fourteen abstaining.[56] It was, therefore, established that amendments to the Covenant could be proposed by a majority vote of the Assembly including the representatives of all the states having membership on the Council. As the amendments here proposed to Article 26 have never received a sufficient number of ratifications to allow them to come into force, the Covenant still permits the proposal of amendments by a majority vote rather than by a three-fourths vote of the Assembly. However, the recommendation that they be proposed only by a three-fourths majority has been renewed from time to time.

Amendments have actually been proposed over the active opposition of members of the Assembly. Toward the end of the session of the Second Assembly the following amendments to Article 6 were proposed:

The expenses of the League shall be borne by the Members of the League in the proportion decided by the Assembly.[57]

The allocation of the expenses of the League set out in Annex 3 shall be applied as from January 1, 1922, until a revised allocation has come into force after adoption by the Assembly.[58]

The resolution proposing the first of these amendments was adopted by a vote of forty for the resolution, one against (Greece) and ten abstaining.[59] The

[56] *Ibid.*, pp. 733, 734, 735.
[57] *Ibid.*, p. 885.
[58] *Ibid.*, p. 886.
[59] *Ibid.*, p. 885.

second was adopted by a vote of thirty-one for the
resolution, two against (Cuba and Uruguay) and
eighteen abstaining.[60]

To the writer it does not appear that the intention
of the framers of the Covenant in regard to the proposal of amendments is open to reasonable doubt. They
did intend that a majority vote of the Assembly, including the votes of all the Council members, should suffice.[61] However, this intention can not be ascertained
from a consideration of the provisions of the Covenant. It is submitted that, if only the language of
the Covenant be examined, and if words be assigned
the meaning normally given to them in such legal
instruments, the *only* conclusion that can be reached is
that unanimity is required for the proposal of amendments. To hold that the " decisions " mentioned in
Article 5, paragraph 1, refers only to resolutions by
which it is intended to impose immediate legal obligations is to give to the word a meaning which it ordinarily does not possess and also one for which there
is no indication whatsoever that the authors of the
Covenant intended it to possess. The action of the
Assembly in deciding to propose an amendment to the
Covenant or in deciding to make a recommendation to
the Council or to the Governments would, if one assign
the normal meaning to the word, be described as " decisions." Yet the Assembly, in order to avoid the necessity of achieving strict unanimity in such cases, holds
that such are not " decisions " within the meaning of
the Covenant.

It also seems significant that the Assembly again
explained the adoption of the unanimity rule in the

---

[60] *Ibid.,* p. 886.
[61] See above, pp. 19-20.

first place as a means of protecting "the rights of state sovereignty," and they further stated that it only needed to be maintained where it served that end. Now if the "rights of sovereignty" may be explained as simply meaning that no state may have an obligation imposed upon it without its prior consent, it is suggested that the amending machinery of the League gives scant protection to those states lacking Council seats. Technically, of course, "sovereignty" is protected by the right of withdrawal. But in reality it is much more probable that self-interest will compel states to remain in the League even though by doing so they become bound by an amendment which they voted against and which they have not ratified. If this worn-out juristic concept, which grew up in a world of a very different character, can be so easily satisfied, the future of the League appears that much brighter.

To the writer, the decision by the Assembly to the effect that "recommendations" can be adopted by majority vote and that amendments can be proposed by a like vote, including, of course, the votes of all those having Council seats, appears to be a very hopeful sign for the success of the League. Not only does it allow recommendations to be made and amendments to be proposed without the consent of all, but it shows a decided disposition on the part of the Members not to allow the unanimity rule to make the League impotent, and this in spite of the explicit provisions of the legal instrument which forms its fundamental law. An examination of the debates in the committees and in the plenary sessions makes it seem clear beyond a doubt that the Assembly was moved to take the position that it did upon "recommendations" and upon the proposal of amendments by viewing the *conse-*

9

quences to which a contrary position would lead, rather than by the weight of the flimsy legal arguments that were advanced to justify the course that the best interests of the League demanded that they pursue.[62]

[62] See particularly the remarks of Mr. Balfour (British Empire), M. Seferiades (Greece), M. Rolin (Belgium), M. Fernandes (Brazil) in the First Committee of the Second Assembly and in the Plenary Session.

CHAPTER V

Modifications of Unanimity Achieved through Practice (*Concluded*)

COMMITTEE PROCEDURE

The Rules of Procedure of the Assembly provide that decisions in the committees as well as in the plenary sessions shall be taken by unanimous vote. That is, Rule 19 lays down the unanimity requirement for the Assembly, except where otherwise expressly provided in the terms of the Covenant or peace treaties, and Rule 27 provides that " the Rules of Procedure shall apply also to the proceedings of the Committees of the Assembly." However, as is so frequently the case in legislative bodies, the Rules of Procedure give a very inaccurate picture of the procedure followed, for the six Assembly committees have from the time of their creation reached decisions, as a general rule, by majority vote. Indeed, in the Fourth Committee, which deals with League finances, the majority principle appears to be established beyond the possibility of challenge. It will be appreciated, of course, that this practice greatly facilitates the working efficiency of the committees and also assists in the circumvention of the unanimity rule in the Assembly itself, for, as will be shown presently, resolutions which have been voted by large majorities in the committees are generally permitted to achieve unanimity in the Assembly.

Careful attention was given by the Fifth Assembly to the question of how decisions should be taken in the Committees. This consideration resulted from a proposal by the Netherlands delegation to amend Article

27 of the Rules of Procedure to provide "that decisions of the Committees shall be taken by the vote of the majority of the Members of the League represented at the meeting."[1] This action by Netherlands appears to be a direct outgrowth of a decision by Chairman Motta (Switzerland) of the First Committee of the Fourth Assembly to the effect that a resolution, sponsored by the Netherlands delegation and pertaining to the election of the non-permanent members of the Council, had not been adopted although it had received eighteen affirmative votes as against five negative and seven abstentions. M. Motta had held that the unanimous vote required by Rules 19 and 27 had not been achieved.[2] M. Loudon (Netherlands) declared that M. Motta's ruling was "not in accordance with the universal practice for voting in Committees."[3]

The Netherlands proposal was submitted by the Assembly to its First Committee for study and that body reported against making any change in the rules in respect to voting in the committees.[4] The committee report setting forth in detail the practice actually followed received the unanimous approval of the Assembly, thus giving official sanction to the practice.[5] This report and the debates in the First Committee and the plenary session supply an excellent picture of the practice actually followed by the committees. It was agreed that the Netherlands amendment merely proposed to change the Rules of Procedure

[1] *Records of the Fifth Assembly,* First Committee, p. 96.
[2] *Records of the Fourth Assembly,* First Committee, p. 39.
[3] *Records of the Fourth Assembly,* Plenary, p. 114.
[4] *Records of the Fifth Assembly,* Plenary, p. 411.
[5] *Ibid.,* p. 113.

to bring them into harmony with the " almost invariable practice of the committees." [6] It was recognized
that the committees had never followed the provisions
of the rules in respect to unanimity, this being justi-
fiable, inasmuch as the decisions of the committees are
not " decisions " in the sense referred to in the Covenant, but are only " a preliminary and provisional stage
of the resolutions finally adopted by the Assembly." [7]

Although the Netherlands amendment would merely
have legalized the practice generally followed, it was
believed that certain disadvantages would result from
its adoption. It was held that it would destroy the
flexibility of the existing system which permitted the
chairman to use his judgment in determining whether
a resolution had been adopted or defeated. When resolutions of a type not requiring unanimity in the Assembly are being dealt with in committee, the chairman,
of course, never insists upon that body achieving unanimous agreement. When dealing with resolutions that
will require unanimity in the Assembly, the committee
chairman must show discretion in deciding whether a
majority vote in the committee suffices or whether to
insist upon unanimity in the committee. As M. Rolin
(Belgium), *rapporteur*, pointed out, in the great majority of cases the presence of negative votes in committee does not mean that unanimity will not be
attained in the Assembly. Delegations finding themselves in a minority are generally " prepared to submit to the will of the majority of the Assembly or at
least to abstain from voting." [8] M. Rolin was of the
opinion that " the contrary is very rarely the case, and
only occurs when the opposition raised during the pro-

[6] *Ibid.*, p. 112.
[7] *Ibid.*, p. 412.
[8] *Ibid.*, p. 112.

ceedings of the committees is absolutely decisive or is due to a profound divergence of views." [9] Thus, as long as the rule requiring unanimity in the committees, as well as in the Assembly proper is retained, committee chairmen can prevent resolutions of the character requiring unanimity from reaching the plenary session when it appears impossible for unanimity to be achieved in that body. On the other hand, when in their judgment it does not seem probable that the minority would go so far as to cast negative votes in the plenary session, majority decisions in the committees can be taken. A perusal of committee minutes has shown the cases in which a resolution has been declared defeated after having received majority endorsement to be exceedingly rare. Indeed, one would not expect them to be of frequent occurrence in view of the fact that the Netherlands delegation had questioned the legality of M. Motta's ruling to that effect. They considered the majority principle to be so well established by committee practice that, in spite of the written rule, unanimity could not be insisted upon. However, it is not unusual for a committee to postpone decision, when the subject permits, in cases in which it appears that only a small majority can be mustered or when the minority appears to be very insistent upon its point of view. Furthermore, when a resolution is presented to the Assembly after having been voted by a bare majority in committee, the Assembly itself may insist upon additional consideration by the committee.[10] Such delay allows further opportunity for a position

[9] *Ibid.*, p. 112.
[10] See, for example, the case in which the Tenth Assembly adjourned for another year consideration of a resolution which had been passed by a 10 to 8 vote of the committee. *Records of the Tenth Assembly,* Plenary, p. 138.

to be found more acceptable to all or to a greater majority.

In order to show that, in actual practice, unanimity is frequently achieved in the Assembly upon resolutions which have been voted by a majority in committee, a few examples will be given. In the Fourth Committee of the Ninth Assembly, the very important resolution providing for the creation of a Supervisory Financial Commission, the members to be named by the Assembly, was adopted by a vote of 13 for to 6 against.[11] The debate indicated that at least one power occupying a permanent Council seat, the British Empire, was included in the minority.[12] However, the resolution was adopted without change by unanimous vote of the Assembly.[13]

In the Third Committee of the Tenth Assembly the draft convention on Financial Assistance in Case of War or Threat of War was opposed by Australia.[14] The convention later received the unanimous vote of the Assembly.[15]

In respect to budgetary questions in the Fourth Committee it may be said that the majority principle has been completely achieved. The very existence of the League has depended, of course, upon this committee being able to make decisions without a single state or a small minority having power to obstruct. Therefore from the outset " a gentleman's agreement " has existed in virtue of which " the minority of the

[11] *Records of the Ninth Assembly*, Fourth Committee, p. 90.

[12] *Ibid.*, p. 89.

[13] *Records of the Ninth Assembly*, Plenary, p. 192.

[14] *Records of the Tenth Assembly*, Third Committee, p. 36.

[15] *Records of the Tenth Assembly*, Plenary, p. 164.

Fourth Committee has always given way to the majority." [16] The legality of such a practice, in view of the provisions of the Assembly Rules of Procedure, is, however, occasionally called in question by representatives who have had budget items adopted over their negative votes. For example, in the Fourth Committee of the Sixth Assembly the Chairman, Dr. Alfonso Augusto da Costa (Portugal) declared to be adopted an item calling for the appropriation of 303,000 francs for the assistance of refugees, even though the delegates of Italy, Japan, Nicaragua, Uruguay and Venezuela had voted against it. [17]

M. Zumeta (Venezuela) stated that in Article 19, paragraph 2, of the Rules of Procedure, certain exceptions were recognized from the general rule of unanimity in the Assembly and Committees. However, he said that he did not find budgetary issues to be among the exceptions mentioned. He asked, therefore, on what legal foundation the practice of passing budgetary items by majority vote rested. [18]

M. Reveillaud (France) replied that " if unanimity were indispensable, the committees would seldom get anything done, and apart from that practical aspect, it was not altogether clear that the Committee's resolutions—mere proposals to the Assembly as they were—were properly to be treated as decisions at all." He further stated that if a delegation could not see its way clear to bow to the majority opinion of the committee it was always at liberty to oppose the vote in the Assembly. " Hence the tacit understanding

---

[16] The words are those of M. Osusky (Czechoslovakia), an experienced member of the Fourth Committee. *Records of the Eighth Assembly, Plenary,* p. 199.

[17] *Records of the Sixth Assembly,* Fourth Committee, p. 60.

[18] *Ibid.,* p. 60.

whereby a dissenting delegation, having explained its point of view, would maintain no formal opposition to the adoption of a budget recommended, even though not unanimously, by the Fourth Committee." [19] The Chairman stated that there was " no doubt that the precedents, of which he had made a careful study, were clearly on the side of M. Reveillaud." [20] M. Zumeta (Venezuela) pointed out that his remarks had been merely to question the law. He understood perfectly what had been assented to in practice. He " merely desired to record his opinion that that assent, however long established the practice might become, would never be anything else but voluntary submission to a plain derogation from the strict requirements of the law." [21]

The item against which five states had voted, including two having permanent Council seats, was thus declared to be adopted by the committee and it subsequently received the unanimous approval of the Assembly.[22]

Occasionally, when a credit has been voted or denied by the vote of a very small majority of the Fourth Committee, the Assembly refuses to give unanimous assent to the resolution submitted. For example, the Fourth Committee of the Eighth Assembly refused a credit of 40,000 francs for the work of a commission of jurists to study the codification of international law. The vote in the committee was seventeen votes against the credit and eleven votes for it.[23] When the budget came before the Assembly M. Vennersten (Sweden)

---

[19] *Ibid.,* p. 60.
[20] *Ibid.,* p. 60.
[21] *Ibid.,* p. 60.
[22] *Records of the Sixth Assembly,* Plenary, p. 153.
[23] *Records of the Eighth Assembly,* Fourth Committee, p. 50.

moved to amend the budget to include this item.[24] It
was pointed out by the President, Dr. Alberto Guani
(Uruguay), that a unanimous vote would be required.[25]
M. Rolin (Belgium), however, stated that an amendment to the budget " which is not unanimously accepted
is not necessarily rejected." If a majority favored the
credit it would be proper to refer it back to the finance
committee for new discussions and proposals.[26] The
vote was taken, the amendment of M. Vennersten
receiving twenty votes for it and seventeen votes
against it.[27] The item in question was thereupon referred back to the Fourth Committee and a way was
found for including the 40,000 francs in the League
budget.

On a previous occasion an attempt had been made
to induce the Assembly to adopt an item that had been
defeated in the Fourth Committee or at least to refer
it back to that committee for further consideration.
The item in question was a supplementary credit of
147,000 gold francs for the High Commissariat for
Refugees (Russian Section). It was refused by the
Fourth Committee of the Fourth Assembly by a vote
of twenty to nine.[28] When the budget came before the
Assembly the delegates of Bulgaria and Roumania
urged its insertion, but their proposal failed by a vote
of twenty-three votes against to sixteen for, with
three abstentions.[29]

Ordinarily credits voted by a majority of the Fourth
Committee are accepted unanimously by the Assembly.
In the case involving the credit of 40,000 francs for

[24] *Records of the Eighth Assembly*, Plenary, p. 195.
[25] *Ibid.*, p. 200.
[26] *Ibid.*, p. 200.
[27] *Journal of the Eighth Assembly*, p. 343.
[28] *Records of the Fourth Assembly*, Fourth Committee, p. 74.
[29] *Records of the Fourth Assembly*, Plenary, p. 137.

the study of the codification of international law, the
item was referred back to the Committee not because
it had been decided upon by a majority vote but because
the Assembly discovered that the Committee's vote in
fact represented only the desires of a minority, owing,
no doubt, to the failure of some states to avail themselves of their privilege of constant representation
upon each of the six great committees.

The budget and budget items which are formulated
in the Fourth Committee often, as has been indicated,
by majority vote, must, of course, receive the unanimous approval of the Assembly. In actual practice
that unanimous approval has never been denied,
although delegations have occasionally threatened to
use their *liberum veto* in such a manner. For example,
in the Ninth Assembly the Earl of Lytton (India),
after stating that the Indian delegation was pro-
foundly dissatisfied with the budget which had been
proposed and with the way in which the proceedings
of the Fourth Committee were conducted, declared:
"Weak as our normal procedure of control may be,
there does exist in the last resort one method by which
a dissentient member may insist upon getting his views
respected. Like all the resolutions of this Assembly,
that which approves the budget requires a unanimous
vote. Therefore I appeal very earnestly to all the delegations here present, to the Secretary-General of the
League, and more especially to the Director of the
International Labor Organization [Lytton had opposed
an increase in the budget of the Labor Organization],
not to force the Indian delegation into the very un-
welcome necessity of refusing to assent to the
budget." [30]

[30] *Records of the Ninth Assembly,* Plenary, p. 188.

Similar threats had been made by the Indian and Persian delegations in the Fourth Assembly.[31] Delegations dissatisfied with the budget frequently show that dissatisfaction by abstaining.[32]

An incident which occurred in the Ninth Assembly will serve to illustrate how completely the majority principle has been approximated in the Assembly itself, as well as in the Fourth Committee, when budgetary questions are under consideration. When the budget of that year was put to a vote Chapter 2, Item 3 was reserved, for it was understood that it was opposed. Just before this item was put to a separate vote M. Hambro (Norway) said:

> I only want to say, and I think I can say this in the names of all those who voted against this item [in the Fourth Committee], that it is not our idea in any way to obstruct it. If it is proved here that there is a majority in favor of the creation of this post [in the International Labor Organization] we will all loyally vote for it.[33]

The vote was taken and announced as eighteen in favor, six against, with eleven abstaining.[34]

Before the President, M. Zahle (Denmark), announced whether the item had been rejected or accepted he spoke as follows:

> I should like to ask M. Hambro whether he was speaking, before the vote was taken, on behalf of his own delegation or on behalf of the others as well.[35]

M. Hambro stated that all the members who constituted the minority were of the same opinion and had no intention of obstructing the item.[36]

[31] *Records of the Fourth Assembly*, Plenary, p. 130.

[32] See, for example, the abstention of Lithuania in the Sixth Assembly. *Records of the Sixth Assembly*, Plenary, p. 145.

[33] *Records of the Ninth Assembly*, Plenary, p. 191.

[34] *Ibid.*, p. 191.

[35] *Ibid.*

[36] *Ibid.*

The President expressed the intention of taking a second vote but M. Motta (Switzerland) said that it was unnecessary, stating that, " Since the six who cast negative votes withdraw their opposition you need merely say that the item has been passed." [37]

After asking each delegation that had cast a negative vote if it had withdrawn its opposition and having received affirmative answers, the President announced that the item had been adopted by a unanimous vote.[38]

This incident is regarded as being of importance as it constituted a clear recognition of the practice that when the majority decides on a question pertaining to the budget the minority must give way in the plenary session as well as in the Fourth Committee.

Some attempt has been made to place the majority principle followed in financial matters in both the Fourth Committee and the Assembly upon a legal basis rather than to allow it to rest entirely upon the voluntary observance of an unwritten rule. In 1921 the Committee on Amendments to the Covenant (London Committee) which had been appointed by the Council suggested the following amendment to Article 6 of the Covenant:

> The Assembly shall vote the annual budget of the League and approve its accounts . . . .
>
> These matters shall be decided by a three-fourths majority in which there shall be included the votes of all the Members of the League represented on the Council.[39]

The Committee did not consider it possible to apply the rule of unanimity to the voting of the budget for " on the voting of the budget depends the whole work-

[37] Ibid.
[38] Ibid.
[39] Committee on Amendments to the Covenant, First Report to the Council, p. 14. (League Doc. A. 24. 1921. V.)

ing of the League; and the risk of compromising its activities through an opposing vote of a small minority of its Members must not be incurred."[40] At the same time, the committee did not believe a simple majority sufficient for so important a matter. They therefore decided upon a three-fourths majority, including all the Council members " as the Council is the executive organ responsible for carrying out the League's activities." The Council could not fulfill this task well unless it had a budget which it had itself approved. Moreover, the committee felt that it was perfectly proper to modify unanimity in this respect for " the voting of the budget cannot be regarded as similar to an ordinary decision for which unanimity is required." [41]

While the practical reasons mentioned in the committee report are of the greatest importance as reasons for not insisting upon unanimity in voting the budget, the attempt to build up a case for holding decisions on the budget as well as decisions on the proposal of amendments and the adoption of recommendations not " decisions " within the meaning of Article 5 appears absurd in the light of the committee's own definition of " decision," for it certainly can not be denied that the budget imposes direct legal obligations upon the member states.

The amendment suggested by the London Committee was referred by the Second Assembly to its First Committee for study. A sub-committee reported favorably upon it and it was enthusiastically supported by M. Noblemaire (France) in the committee itself. M. Noblemaire declared that " if there was a question which required to be dealt with in a practical spirit it was the question of money " and that " if unanimity

[40] *Ibid.*, p. 14.
[41] *Ibid.*

were insisted upon, money would not be forthcoming." [42] M. Fernandes (Brazil) was, however, of the opinion that " there was no question which more fully justified the demand for unanimity than this important question of financial control." [43] M. Motta (Switzerland) suggested that the amendment not be pushed as " it was impossible not to apply it, even if it was not explicity laid down in the Covenant." [44] The Chairman, M. Scialoja (Italy) expressed himself as in agreement with M. Motta, pointing out that, should the amendment be rejected in the Assembly or by the Governments, it might be a serious argument against the practice already followed in the Assembly.[45] M. Noblemaire (France) accepted the views of M. Motta and M. Scialoja and the proposed amendment to Article 6 was not reported to the Assembly. The wisdom of M. Motta's view has been demonstrated by subsequent events as budget practice has grown up much as he predicted.

During the consideration of the budget by the Third Assembly a ruling was made by President Augustin Edwards (Chile) which caused some attention to be devoted to the subject by the Council. The incident also serves to demonstrate how firmly fixed the majority principle had become even as early as 1922. A resolution had been introduced in the plenary session calling for an increase of 50,000 francs in the appropriation for the Committee on Intellectual Cooperation. The resolution was put to the vote and twenty-five delegations voted for it, twelve against it, [46] and nine

[42] *Records of the Second Assembly,* First Committee, p. 99.
[43] *Ibid.*
[44] *Ibid.,* p. 100.
[45] *Ibid.*
[46] The negative votes were cast by Australia, British Empire, Canada, China, Denmark, Esthonia, Netherlands, New Zealand, Norway,

were absent or abstained.[47] The resolution was declared
by the President to have been adopted even though
twelve states, including one power having a permanent
Council seat, had voted against it. In accordance with
a resolution adopted by the Third Assembly, the question of the procedure to be followed in the adoption of
the budget was submitted to the Council for study.
The Council submitted the question to M. Tang
Tsai-Fou (China) for study and report. His report was
in part as follows:

The question is primarily a legal one. Can a resolution including
a credit in the budget of the League be adopted by a vote of the
majority of the Assembly, or is unanimity required? When this question has been answered the question may arise as to what is the best
procedure for the Assembly to adopt in dealing with budgetary
proposals.

It appears . . . . that there is no precedent, previous to the
decision of the President of the Third Assembly, in favor of the view
that a budgetary proposal can be adopted by a majority vote of
the Assembly. The principal argument for such a view is the practical argument that it may be difficult to carry on the work of the
League if the granting of necessary credits can be prevented by the
opposition of a single member. The legal objections against holding
that a majority vote suffices appear, however, to be serious. The
budget adopted by the Assembly determines the amount of money
which each Member of the League is to contribute towards its expenses, and the vote adopting the budget is, therefore, a vote impos-
ing a liability upon the Members of the League. It may be maintained that an explicit provision of the Covenant would be necessary
to authorize a majority of the Members of the League to impose upon
the other members a financial liability from which they expressly
dissented. The Covenant contains no such provisions. On the contrary, it contains, in Article 5, the rule that all decisions of the

Panama, Siam and South Africa. (*Records of the Third Assembly,*
Plenary, p. 368.)

[47] The absent or abstaining states were Austria, Chile, Colombia,
Latvia, Luxemburg, Paraguay, Sweden, Switzerland, and Uruguay.
(*Records of the Third Assembly,* Plenary, p. 369.)

Assembly or Council shall require the agreement of all the Members of the League represented at the meeting, except where the contrary is expressly stated.[48]

M. Tsai-Fou went on to suggest, however, that the question was one which should properly be dealt with by the Assembly itself.[49] This view was accepted by the Council and, in accordance therewith, they adopted a resolution suggesting that the question be placed upon the agenda of the Fourth Assembly.[50]

Apparently, however, the Assembly came to the conclusion that it would be better to avoid an explicit commitment on the question, for instead of referring it to the First Committee, where questions of a legal or constitutional nature normally go, it was referred to the General Committee.[51] No report upon the question was ever made to the Assembly.

By way of summary, it may be said that, although the Assembly Rules of Procedure specifically require unanimity in the committees, except in dealing with certain specified questions, unanimity is seldom insisted upon. Indeed, in the Fourth Committee it is never insisted upon. Resolutions which receive the support of large majorities in committees other than the Fourth may normally be expected to achieve unanimity in the Assembly, probably with several delegations expressing their disapproval by abstaining. The budget or budget items voted by an actual majority in the Fourth Committee have always achieved unanimity (or at least have always been declared adopted) in the Assembly. Legally, it appears that a dissatisfied delegation could

---

[48] *O. J.*, 1923, p. 245.
[49] *Ibid.*, p. 246.
[50] *Ibid.*, p. 199.
[51] *Records of the Fourth Assembly*, Plenary, p. 21.

10

cast a negative vote defeating the resolution, and occasionally such a threat is made. Practice, however, seems to indicate that such an action is exceedingly improbable.

THE RIGHT OF PARTIES TO A DISPUTE TO VOTE

How far are Members of the League permitted under the Covenant to be judges in their own cause? Are the votes of the parties to be counted in the settlement of disputes and in the determination of steps to be taken in carrying out the terms of such settlements? Article 15, paragraphs 6, 7, and 10, and Article 16, paragraph 4, expressly specify that the votes of the parties concerned are not to be counted in determining whether the vote specified by the Covenant has been attained. On the other hand, Article 10, Article 11, Article 13 and Article 19 make no mention of the exclusion of the parties. From a consideration of the text of the Covenant alone one might reasonably conclude that only in the four cases cited are the votes of the interested parties to be excluded. It might also appear that the omission of all reference in other parts of the Covenant to the votes of the parties in dispute resulted from a deliberate attempt on the part of the authors of the Covenant to emphasize the requirement of absolute unanimity.

There is, however, ample evidence to show that such was not the intention of those who drafted the Covenant. For instance, President Wilson did not believe that absolute unanimity was essential for the Council to " advise upon " the means by which the obligations of Article 10 were to be fulfilled. In his conference with the members of the Foreign Relations Committee of the Senate in August, 1919, he spoke of Article 10 as follows:

Article 10 is in no respect of doubtful meaning when read in the light of the Covenant as a whole. The Council of the League can only advise upon the means by which the obligations of that great article are to be given effect to. *Unless the United States is a party to the policy or action in question,* her own affirmative vote in the Council is necessary before any advice can be given, for a unanimous vote of the Council is required.[52]

In addition there is the testimony of Lord Robert Cecil and M. Scialoja, both of whom were members of the League of Nations Commission, which was given in 1930 in the Committee for the Amendment of the Covenant to bring it into harmony with the Paris Pact. Both stated that sheer oversight explains the fact that in some cases the Covenant excludes the votes of the parties to a dispute and in other cases does not.[53] Both men were clearly of the opinion that absolute unanimity is not essential under Article 13, paragraph 4, of the Covenant.

The situation confronting the League in respect to the determination of whether the votes of parties to a dispute should be excluded in cases other than the four mentioned specifically in the Covenant appears similar to that which it faced in respect to the proposal of amendments. It will be recalled that in the latter case strict adherence to the text of the Covenant would have necessitated requiring unanimity for the proposal of amendments, although such an interpretation would have run counter to the intentions of the authors of

[52] *Senate Document No. 76,* 66th Congress, First Session. Italics added.

[53] *Minutes of the Committee for the Amendment of the Covenant of the League of Nations in order to Bring It into Harmony with the Pact of Paris,* pp. 47-48. (League Doc. C. 160. M. 69. 1930. V.)

the document as shown by the minutes of the League of Nations Commission and by the subsequent statements of several of its members; and, what is of greater importance, it would have saddled the League with an amending process of such a difficult nature as to make the development of the League by means of amendments to the Covenant virtually impossible. Much the same situation confronts the League in the case under consideration. The statements of Wilson, Cecil, and Scialoja indicate that it was not the intention of the authors to require absolute unanimity in *all* cases other than those mentioned, yet strict adherence to the terms of the Covenant would lead one to that conclusion. Moreover, to interpret the document in this manner would make certain articles otherwise of great importance practically worthless, for if a decision can not be deemed unanimous without the votes of the parties to the dispute or without the vote of a party against whom a settlement is to be executed, then unanimity becomes difficult to achieve. Indeed, it becomes so difficult that it leads to an absurdity, for it would mean, for instance, that under Article 16, paragraph 2, the measures recommended to be taken against an " aggressor " could not be legally valid unless the " aggressor " voted for them. This result is made doubly certain by the provisions of Article 4, paragraph 5, and Article 17, which guarantee the parties Council seats during the consideration of disputes in which they are involved in case they do not already occupy such seats.

In regard to the problem of the proposal of amendments, the League discovered a convenient way out of the difficulty, namely, by holding that the decision to propose an amendment was not a " decision " within the meaning of Article 5 of the Covenant. Thus, instead of giving Article 26 a strict interpretation in accordance with the words of the article, it was interpreted in accordance with the intentions of the authors and in accordance with what was deemed by the members of the Assembly to be for the best interests of the League. A similar way out appears to exist in respect to the problem of deciding under what circumstances the votes of the parties to a dispute or the vote of a party against whom a settlement is to be executed are to be counted. The effects of this acknowledged flaw in the wording of the Covenant might be avoided by an interpretation made in the light of a long recognized principle of general law.[54] That is, the principle of law by which it is decreed that no one is permitted to be a judge in his own cause might be given priority over an interpretation based upon strict adherence to the wording of the Covenant.

A survey of the practice of the League organs will show that the course that they have pursued has, by no means, been entirely consistent in respect to the problem here discussed. They do not appear to have chosen one path and rejected the other but rather to have wavered between them. In certain instances they seem to have been guided by a strict adherence to the words of the Covenant, and in other cases they appear to have construed that document in a more liberal manner. A consideration of the decisions and debates in respect to the votes of the parties to disputes will serve to indicate the nature and the extent of the precedents which have been formed, some pointing in one direction and some in another. It is hoped that this may be of some value as a basis for predicting the course which will ultimately be followed by the League.

[54] Compare H. Lauterpacht, "Japan and the Covenant," in *The Political Quarterly*, III, No. 2.

First, a survey will be made of the evidence which seems to suggest that it has been the intention of the League to apply the rule of law that no one shall be judge in his own cause. It should be understood, of course, that this principle can be applied just as logically to decisions on the execution of a settlement as to the taking of the decision on the dispute itself, for in neither case could the party or parties concerned be expected to vote in a disinterested fashion.

Perhaps the most impressive pronouncement on the question by a League organ was that of the Permanent Court of International Justice in its advisory opinion given in 1925 on the questions arising in connection with the Iraq boundary dispute between Great Britain and Turkey. The Council had asked the advice of the Court on the nature of the decision they should take in virtue of Article 3, paragraph 2, of the Treaty of Lausanne, whether the decision should be by unanimous or majority vote, and whether the representatives of the interested parties should take part in the vote. The unanimous response of the Court to the final question was in part as follows:

It should be observed that the very general rule laid down in Article 5 of the Covenant does not specially contemplate the case of an actual dispute which has been laid before the Council. On the other hand, this contingency is dealt with in Article 15, paragraphs 6 and 7, which, whilst making the limited binding effect of recommendations dependent on unanimity, explicitly states that the Council's unanimous report need only be agreed to by the Members thereof other than the representatives of the parties. The same principle is applied in the cases contemplated in paragraph 4 of Article 16 of the Covenant and in the first of the three paragraphs which, in accordance with a resolution of the Second Assembly, are to be inserted between the first and second paragraphs of that article.

It follows from the foregoing that, according to the Covenant itself, in certain cases and more particularly in the case of a settlement of a dispute unanimity is applicable, subject to the limitation that the votes cast by representatives of the interested parties do not affect the required unanimity.

The Court is of the opinion that it is this conception of the rule of unanimity which must be applied in the dispute before the Council . . . .

The principle laid down by the Covenant in paragraphs 6 and 7 of Article 15, seems to meet the requirements of a case such as that now before the Council, just as well as the circumstances contemplated in that article. The well-known rule that no one can be judge in his own suit holds good.

From a practical standpoint, to require that the representatives of the parties should accept the Council's decision would be tantamount to giving them a right of veto enabling them to prevent any decision being reached; this would hardly be in conformity with the intention manifested in Article 3, paragraph 2, of the Treaty of Lausanne.

Lastly, it may perhaps be well to observe that since the Council consists of representatives of States or Members, the legal position of the representatives of the parties upon the Council is not comparable to that of national arbitrators upon Courts of Arbitration.

The votes of the representatives of the parties are not, therefore, to be taken into account in ascertaining whether there is unanimity. But the representatives will take part in the vote, for they form part of the Council and, like the other representatives, they are entitled and are in duty bound to take part in the deliberations of that body. The terms of paragraphs 6 and 7 of Article 15 of the Covenant and of the new clause to be inserted in Article 16, clearly show that in cases therein contemplated, the representatives of the parties may take part in the voting, and that it is only for the purpose of determining whether unanimous agreement has been reached that their votes are not counted.[55]

This pronouncement by the Court appears to be one of great importance. To be sure, it was an advisory opinion having no force of law behind it. Moreover, it contains no statements which can be definitely interpreted as a blanket endorsement of the scheme by which it is suggested that the flaws in the wording of the Covenant can be corrected by giving recognized

[55] *Permanent Court of International Justice,* Advisory Opinion No. 12, p. 31.

legal principles priority over technical rules of interpretation in determining the meaning of the Covenant. Instead, it merely holds that, in settling a dispute arising under Article 3, paragraph 2, of the Treaty of Lausanne, it would be proper for the Council to employ the procedure laid down in Article 15, paragraphs 6 and 7. There is nothing to indicate whether the Court would have expressed a similar opinion had the case arisen under Article 11 or some other article of the Covenant which makes no mention of excluding the votes of the parties.

However, this opinion appears important for several reasons. First, it supplies an opening wedge for holding that the votes of the parties should under certain circumstances not be counted in determining whether the requisite vote has been attained; for if it is proper that the votes of the parties be not counted in a dispute arising under Article 3, paragraph 2, of the Treaty of Lausanne, it would also seem to be proper that the votes of the parties be not counted in all similar cases where no treaty or Covenant provision is found to the contrary. In the second place, it is significant that the opening so made is not closed. There is no suggestion that in *only* such cases should the Council depart from absolute unanimity. Moreover, the opinion brings out the absurdity of expecting that decisions can be made with a requirement of absolute unanimity. This suggests that additional inroads upon the doctrine of strict unanimity in the settling of disputes and in the application of the terms of settlements should be made. Perhaps the authors of the opinion did not intend to suggest that such inroads can be made by giving priority to the legal rule that no one can be judge in his own cause. On the other hand, the

Court did not imply the contrary. The path for such an interpretation was allowed by the Court to remain open.

To a certain extent, this advisory opinion did not break new ground, for on several occasions prior to 1925 both the Assembly and the Council had shown an inclination to exclude the votes of the parties to a dispute.

As early as 1921 the Assembly recognized that certain parts of the Covenant would, indeed, be weak if it were held that the votes of the parties should be counted in all cases in which they were not specifically excluded. In order to make certain that the application of Article 16 could not be prevented by such an interpretation, the following amendment to that Article, proposed by the Third Committee, was adopted by the Second Assembly:

It is for the Council to give an opinion whether or not a breach of the Covenant has taken place. In deliberations on this question in the Council, the votes of Members of the League alleged to have resorted to war and of Members against whom such action was directed shall not be counted.[56]

This proposed amendment has not become a part of the Covenant as it has not yet been ratified to the extent required by Article 26. However, at the time the amendment was proposed by the Second Assembly, they adopted a resolution recommending that, pending the ratification of the amendment, the votes of the parties be excluded in determining whether unanimity had in fact been achieved.[57]

In 1922 the Council definitely recognized that when it fulfills a judicial function the votes of the interested

---

[56] *Records of the Second Assembly,* Plenary, p. 443.
[57] *Ibid.,* p. 450.

parties should not count. This occurred in connection
with the fulfillment by the Council of a function given
to it by Article 393 of the Treaty of Versailles, namely,
that of designating those eight states of chief industrial importance for purposes of representation on
the Governing Body of the International Labor Organization. India demanded under Article 4 of the Covenant the right of full Council membership during the
consideration of her claim for designation as one of
the eight states of chief industrial importance.[58] The
Council asked the Director of the Legal Section of the
Secretariat, Dr. Van Hamel, whether in his opinion
" India might be represented on the Council with the
right to vote, in conformity with Article 4 of the
Covenant, or whether the Council would sit, when dealing with this subject as in some sense a court of arbitration." [59] His reply was that " the Council would
act in this affair as arbitrator, and that India could
not be both judge and party to the case." [60] The Council endorsed this view, thus giving recognition to and
acting upon the legal principle that parties can not
be permitted to sit as judges in their own case, several
years before the Court rendered its advisory opinion
upon the subject.

In the settlement of the boundary dispute between
Austria and Hungary in 1922, the Council again acted
upon this principle. The memorandum of the Secretary-General prepared for the Council on the " legal
considerations " involved in the case contained the
following statement:

Austria, having declared by the Protocol of Venice " that she
would accept a decision recommended by the Council of the League

---

[58] *O. J.*, 1922, p. 1160.
[59] *Ibid.*
[60] *Ibid.*

of Nations," must not take part in the vote, but will at the same time be represented at discussions of the Council in virtue of Article 4 of the Covenant, which provides that "any member of the League not represented on the Council shall be invited to send a representative to sit as a member at any meeting of the Council during the consideration of matters specially affecting the interests of that Member of the League." [61]

The principle was likewise followed in settling the boundary between Czechoslovakia and Hungary. The two parties concerned had agreed to submit the question to the Council for arbitration, the President informing them that the decision would, therefore, be obligatory.[62] The decision was taken by a unanimous vote of the Council exclusive of the parties.[63] The parties were subsequently notified of the Council decision at a public meeting of the Council.[64]

The precedent established in the cases which have been cited was further strengthened in 1924. At this time the Council decided to conduct its investigations concerning the fulfillment of the military terms of the peace treaties without granting representation to states subject to the investigations.[65] As a result of this decision the Hungarian Minister at Rome sent a letter of protest to the President of the Council. This unavailing protest serves to bring out admirably the theory upon which the Council was acting. It read in part as follows:

The principle that no one can be his own judge does not justify, in the case in point, the exclusion of the States subject to control. Although this principle applies in jurisprudence, it is not applicable to the Council of the League of Nations; such an application would

---

[61] *Ibid.*, p. 1333.
[62] *O. J.*, 1923, p. 209.
[63] *Ibid.*, p. 599.
[64] *Ibid.*, p. 601.
[65] *O. J.*, 1924, p. 1340.

singularly distort the idea on which the League is based, and would, in fact, be tantamount to the abolition of the sovereignty of its Members.[66]

The case for the exclusion of the votes of parties to the dispute was greatly strengthened by the action of the Council in the famous Greco-Bulgar dispute of 1925 coming before the Council under Articles 10 and 11—articles which make no provision for the exclusion of the votes of the parties. The Council, without the representatives of Greece and Bulgaria, prepared a " dictatorial request " which was submitted to the parties for their acceptance.[67] The Council then assembled in a public meeting and the President, M. Briand (France) asked first the representative of Bulgaria, M. Marfoff, and then the representative of Greece, M. Carapanos, whether they had any objections to offer. M. Marfoff said that " he was authorized to declare that his Government was ready to comply unconditionally with the *decision* of the Council of the League of Nations which had just been communicated." [68] M. Carapanos said that he had no objection and that " he would be bound to forward the terms of the *decision* of the Council to his Government which would, he was convinced, comply with them." [69] The resolution was then put to a vote and unanimously adopted.

In actual fact the resolution had been prepared and agreed upon without the representatives of Greece and Bulgaria. The representatives of both countries in referring to it had spoken of the *decision* of the Council. It seems, therefore, that the resolution was put to

[66] *O. J.*, 1925, p. 231.
[67] Compare Conwell-Evans, *The League Council in Action*, pp. 48-60.
[68] *O. J.*, 1925, p. 1700. Italics added.
[69] *Ibid.*, p. 1700. Italics added.

a vote in the public meeting for the purpose of ascertaining whether the two parties were willing to comply with the terms of the resolution rather than to see if the resolution had in fact been adopted. Neither the parties to the dispute nor the other members of the Council appear to have believed that the resolution could be shorn of the moral and legal force which attaches to a unanimous pronouncement of the Council by one or both of the parties to the dispute voting against it.

In 1926, in the course of the debates of the Preparatory Commission for the Disarmament Conference, it was definitely asserted by M. Paul-Boncour (France) that the Council had recognized in a manner beyond dispute that the unanimity required under Article 11 was unanimity exclusive of the votes of the interested parties. He stated that " he did not know whether any lawyers would be found to give such an interpretation " but that " the necessities of life must take precedence over the interpretations of lawyers." For if it was held that the unanimity requirement was not satisfied without the affirmative votes of the parties under Article 11, as it was under Article 15, " the Council would be rendered inoperative, as there would always be one of the two parties who would make unanimity impossible." He further declared that it was accordingly necessary, until further notice, to admit " that preventive measures were subject to the unanimity rule with the exclusion of the interested parties." [70] This expression of opinion on the part of M. Paul-Boncour was not directly challenged by any member of the Commission, although Viscount Cecil (British Empire) took occa-

[70] *Documents of the Preparatory Commission for the Disarmament Conference.* Series 3, p. 71. (League Doc. C. 740. M. 279. 1926 IX.)

sion to point out that it was only Article 15 and not Article 11 which specifically excluded the votes of the interested parties.[71]

Although the report of the Committee of the Council on Article 11, approved by the Council June 15, 1927, does not state precisely that the votes of the interested parties are excluded under that Article, it strongly implies it. Paragraphs " f " and " g " in the section of the report dealing with measures that the Council may adopt in cases in which there is an imminent threat of war read as follows:

(f) Should any of the parties to the dispute disregard the advice or recommendations of the Council, the Council will consider the measures to be taken. It may manifest its formal disapproval. It may also recommend to its Members to withdraw all their diplomatic representatives accredited to the State in question, or certain categories of them. It may also recommend other measures of a more serious character.

(g) If the State in default still persists in its hostile preparations or action, further warning measures may be taken, such as a naval demonstration. Naval demonstrations have been employed for such a purpose in the past. It is possible that air demonstrations might within reasonable limits be employed. Other measures may be found suitable according to the circumstances of the case.[72]

As it seems highly unlikely, to say the least, that a state would consent to a naval or air demonstration against itself, it is clearly assumed here that the votes of the parties are not to be counted in determining whether unanimity has been achieved.

In the same year the Council acted in accordance with this theory in adopting a resolution dealing with the Hungarian Optants dispute between Hungary and Roumania which was before the Council under Article 11, paragraph 2, of the Covenant. In summing up the

[71] *Ibid.*, p. 71.
[72] *O. J.*, 1927, p. 833.

procedure followed by the Council in reaching its decision, the President, M. Villegas (Chile), spoke as follows:

> I proposed that the Council should pronounce on the recommendations contained in that part of the report which I have indicated, but I deliberately excepted two members of the Council who are parties to the dispute.[73]

Thus the Council adopted in this case a resolution embodying a recommendation to the parties by a unanimous vote exclusive of the votes of M. Titulesco (Roumania) and Count Apponyi (Hungary), the representatives of the interested parties.[74]

In 1928 it was again assumed that decisions under Article 11 could be taken by unanimity not including the votes of the interested parties. The question arose this time in the Committee on Security and Arbitration in connection with the German proposal to strengthen Article 11 by giving the Council power to impose an armistice which would be legally binding upon the disputants. In submitting the proposal to discussion, M. Rolin-Jaequemyns (Belgium), *rapporteur*, asked the question, " should the Council's resolutions . . . . be adopted unanimously, not counting of course the representatives of the parties to the dispute, or would a majority vote, simple or qualified, be admissible? " [75] The committee decided in favor of unanimity but it appeared to be clearly understood that the unanimity would not necessarily have to be absolute but might rather be exclusive of the votes of the parties.

[73] *Ibid.*, p. 1413.
[74] *Ibid.*, p. 1414.
[75] *Documents of the Preparatory Commission for the Disarmament Conference:* Minutes of the Third Session of the Committee on Arbitration and Security, p. 38. (League Doc. C. 358. M. 112. 1928 IX.)

If one considered only the decisions and discussions
of the problem cited above, it would appear that the
League had adopted or was, at least, well on its way
to adopt the common-sense rule that the negative vote
of a party can not invalidate a decision which receives
an otherwise unanimous affirmative vote, even though
the Covenant article under which the Assembly or
Council is acting does not so state. However, on at least
two occasions, both of which arose under Article 11
of the Covenant, the Council has ruled that the negative
vote of a party to the dispute is sufficient to deprive
the resolution of all legal force.

Such a decision was made by the Council in 1928 in
a dispute between Lithuania and Poland concerning
the expulsion of Polish nationals from Lithuanian territory. The following resolution had been submitted to
the Council by the President, M. Aguero (Cuba) :

The Council notes the information contained in the report of the
representative of the Netherlands, approves the conclusions of the
report and,

Considering that for the negotiations between Poland and Lithuania to have the successful results indicated in its resolution of
December 10, 1927, it is important that these negotiations should,
before the next session of the Council, have made appreciable
progress,

Asks the representative of the Netherlands to submit a report at its
next session in order that the Council may, if necessary, take up
the question again.[76]

M. Voldemaras (Lithuania) suggested an amendment to this resolution, the amendment receiving the
affirmative vote only of its sponsor.[77] The resolution
in the form here given was then put to a vote and all
voted for it except the representative of Lithuania,

[76] *O. J.*, 1928, p. 893.
[77] *Ibid.*, p. 896.

who voted against it.[78] The President thereupon declared the resolution to have been defeated. Sir Austen Chamberlain (British Empire) expressed himself as being in agreement with this ruling by the President.

During the consideration of the Sino-Japanese dispute submitted to the Council by China under Article 11 of the Covenant, it was again held that a resolution which did not receive a unanimous vote, including the votes of the interested parties, possessed no legal force. The resolution in question was that of October 24, which called upon the Japanese Government " to begin immediately and to proceed progressively with the withdrawal of its troops into the railway zone, so that the total withdrawal may be effected before the date fixed for the next meeting of the Council [Novemvember 16, 1931]." [79]

When the resolution was put to a vote thirteen members were recorded in favor and one (Japan) against.[80] Although the President of the Council, M. Briand (France), declared the draft resolution to have been " adopted unanimously, except for one vote—that of our colleague, the Japanese representative," it seems clear from the statements that followed that neither M. Briand nor the other members of the Council considered the resolution to have anything more than moral force. M. Briand, for example, declared that he still ventured " to hope that, between now and November 16, the evacuation, already begun, will be continued." [81] Had Briand assigned legal force to the resolution, Japan would have been obliged, according to the terms of the Covenant, to which she had sub-

[78] *Ibid.*, p. 896.
[79] *Ibid.*, 1931, p. 2341.
[80] *Ibid.*, p. 2358.
[81] *Ibid.*, p. 2359.

11

scribed, to have completed evacuation by the date mentioned. Moreover, Briand stated that the resolution of September 30 was still to be regarded as in effect.[82] Had the resolution of October 24 been considered as possessing legal force it would have superseded that of September 30. No member of the Council challenged the interpretation placed upon the resolution by M. Briand. In a letter to the President of the Council, dated November 7, 1931, M. Yoshizawa (Japan) declared that, inasmuch as the resolution of October 24 had been opposed by Japan, no resolution was in fact adopted on that date.[83]

What conclusions can be drawn from this survey of decisions and discussions pertaining to circumstances under which the League organs may properly disregard the votes of the interested parties in determining whether the unanimity required by the Covenant has been achieved?

[82] *Ibid.*, p. 2359.

[83] *Ibid.*, p. 2516. (League Doc. C 814. M. 404. 1931 VII.) It is interesting to note, however, that when the Council was considering the Hungarian Optants dispute, submitted to the Council by Hungary under Article 11, the Japanese representative in the Council, M. Adatci, had taken a very different view of the wisdom of allowing the negative vote of an interested party to prevent the adoption of a resolution. After the Roumanian delegate had repeatedly blocked action on the part of the Council, M. Adatci declared that unless some procedure could be found " which would give some hope of success in future negotiations, he was unable to accept the duties of *rapporteur* since it would not be compatible either with his dignity or that of his country to do so." (*O. J.*, 1923, p. 611.) M. Adatci appeared to be in complete agreement with M. Lukacs (Hungary) who declared that it should " be entirely illegal for a person to be at once a party in, and judge of, his own case, and it would not be proper nor in accordance with the dignity of the League of Nations to give the impression that it is possible to settle a dispute between two states by allowing them to vote in their own case." (*Ibid.*, p. 606.)

First, it has been recognized almost from the birth of the League to the present time that the votes of the interested parties would have to be excluded in more cases than the Covenant specifically mentioned if the League was to be as effective as its sponsors desired. This is shown by the amendment proposed to Article 16 by the Second Assembly, by the recommendation adopted by that body, by the advisory opinion of the World Court in the Mossul Affair, by the Council report and discussions on Article 11 and by the discussions and resolutions in the Committee on Amendments to the Covenant to bring it into harmony with the Pact of Paris, all of which have been mentioned above. Further evidence of the need for excluding the votes of the interested parties may be found in the provisions of many of the agreements drawn up between states members of the League since the adoption of the Covenant.[84] Moreover, numerous Council decisions show a willingness to apply the rule of law that no one can be judge in his own cause rather than to rely upon a literal interpretation of the Covenant.

In the second place, it appears highly probable that, whenever the Council is called upon to act in a judicial capacity under the terms of an international instrument other than the Covenant or one of the treaties coming within the provisions of Article 5, the votes of the interested parties will be excluded even though no specific statement to that effect is found. This would merely be acting in accordance with the advisory opinion of the World Court rendered in connection with the Iraq boundary case.

Finally, it appears probable that in the future the Council and Assembly when acting in a strictly judicial

[84] See below, p. 162 ff.

capacity will exclude the votes of the interested parties even when acting under the terms of Covenant articles which make no specific provision for such exclusion. It has no doubt been observed that, in all those cases in which the Council has definitely excluded the votes of the interested parties, the Council has been performing a judicial function. For example, in the case in which India was denied a Council vote in 1922, it was emphasized that the Council was acting as a "court of arbitration." In the boundary disputes between Austria and Hungary, and between Hungary and Czechoslovakia, in 1922 and 1923, respectively, it was again recognized that the Council was in a position to give obligatory decisions inasmuch as the parties had given prior consent to such a procedure. Here again the Council was acting as an arbitral body rather than functioning in the purely political capacity of a mediator. In the Greco-Bulgar dispute the Council was faced with a situation in which one party was using force against the other. The function of the Council was again judicial, for it was obliged to determine whether those acts constituted violations of the obligations previously assumed by the parties and, if so, how the *status quo ante* could be restored. Since the Council was acting in a judicial capacity, the decision was taken, as in the earlier cases, without the votes of the parties. On the other hand, in the dispute between Lithuania and Poland in 1928, in the course of which a Council resolution was defeated by the negative vote of Lithuania, the Council was functioning in a political capacity. It had placed at the disposal of the two parties "the good offices of the League and its organizations" and had in no sense attempted to act as an arbitrator in the dispute. Hence, the ruling of the President to the effect that the resolution had been defeated can scarcely be held a retrogressive step as the Council had never previously held that, while functioning in a political capacity, the votes of the parties are excluded.

However, the defeat of the resolution of October 24, 1931, appears to be in direct conflict with the practice established by the Council, for the Council was in this instance called upon to decide whether certain acts were in violation of existing law and to recommend measures for the restoration of the *status quo ante,* much as it had been in the Greco-Bulgar case of 1925. Thus the Council appears to have been acting in a judicial capacity rather than in the political capacity of a mediator. Therefore the failure of the Council to insist that the resolution of October 24 had been adopted in spite of the negative vote of Japan constituted a retrogressive step, but a retrogressive step for which it is not difficult to supply a motive. For had the Council interpreted the resolution of October 24 as having been legally adopted it would have been virtually obliged, in the event of Japan's failure to act in accordance with its terms, to have recommended to the Governments the use of the sanctions provided in Article 16 of the Covenant.

When the Council, acting in a judicial capacity, is again faced with the necessity of ruling on the question of whether the votes of the interested parties are essential for unanimity, it will have a choice between following the precedent established by the Council which dealt with the Sino-Japanese dispute or of following those earlier precedents which the Council sitting in the autumn of 1931 had ignored. In view of the resourcefulness that the League has displayed in avoiding the rigors of unanimity in the proposal of amendments, in the voting of the budget, and in adopting recommendations to the governments or League organs, it can not reasonably be expected that the Council will continue to allow itself to be made impotent by the requirement of absolute unanimity when acting in a judicial capacity. Moreover, the very prestige of the League, and more particularly that of the Council, demands that the gaps in the Covenant uncovered by Japan be speedily filled. It would be possible to do this by formal amendments to the Covenant. However, the easier method and, for that reason the one more likely to be pursued, is for future Councils to disregard the holding of the Council in the Sino-Japanese dispute and to revert for precedent to those earlier Council decisions in which application was given to the rule of law that no one can be judge in his own cause.

Although the discussions within the League concerning the circumstances in which the votes of the interested parties are to be excluded and the precedents actually established have pertained chiefly to Articles 11, 13, and 16, the principle finally adopted must also apply in cases arising under Articles 10 and 19. It would seem that the Council in expressing an opinion on the applicability of Article 10 and the Assembly in advising the reconsideration of a treaty under Article 19 would be acting in a judicial capacity. Indeed, it has even been asserted by the Institute of International Law that the Council can pronounce by majority vote an opinion on whether an occasion has arisen for the guarantee of Article 10 to become operative.[85] This conclusion appears to have been reached by means of a very literal interpretation of the English text of the article, which provides that " the Council shall advise upon the means by which this obligation shall be ful-

[85] *Records of the Fourth Assembly,* First Committee, p. 56.

filled," and by applying to it the Assembly practice of adopting by majority vote propositions which do not impose legal obligations. However, the case for majority action under Article 10 is weakened by three factors. In the first place, Wilson's explanation of Article 10 made to the members of the Senate Foreign Relations Committee shows clearly that it was the intention of the framers of the Covenant to require unanimity exclusive of the votes of the parties for the application of this Article.[86] In the second place, the French text provides that "*le Council avise aux moyens d'assurer l'exécution de cette obligation*"—a wording which appears to impose something more in the nature of an obligation upon the states than does the English. Finally, the Council, as the report of the London Committee indicated, has never shown any disposition to adopt the Assembly practice of passing recommendations by a majority. It does not, therefore, seem reasonable to expect that if Article 10 is ever invoked against an aggressor state it will be done by majority vote of the Council.

However, in respect to Article 19 the case is quite different. Here the English and French texts are in closer agreement, the one stating that "the Assembly may from time to time advise the reconsideration by the Members of the League of treaties which have become inapplicable" and the other that "*L'Assemblée peut, de temps à autre, inviter les Members de la Société à procéder à un nouvel examen des Traités devenues inapplicables.*" Neither suggests that the Assembly action would impose a legal obligation upon the Members to act in accordance with the resolution adopted. In view of the definitely established Assembly practice of

[86] See above, p. 134.

adopting by majority vote resolutions which do not
impose legal obligations, it would seem that propositions submitted under this article could be adopted by
majority vote. As the principle that no one can be
judge in his own cause should apply just as logically
to decisions taken by majority vote as to decisions taken
by unanimous vote, it would seem that the vote under
this article should be taken by a majority exclusive of
the votes of the parties.

However, the Assembly itself has made no pronouncement on either of the questions involved; that
is, on whether a unanimous vote or only a majority
vote is required and on whether the votes of the interested parties are excluded in determining whether the
requisite vote has been achieved. A committee of jurists
headed by M. Scialoja (Italy), appointed by the Second
Assembly as a result of the application of Bolivia to
have a treaty with Chile " reconsidered," skillfully
avoided touching upon the question of the vote necessary to advise the reconsideration of treaties. Although
M. Edwards (Chile) declared in the Assembly that
absolute unanimity was required for advising that a
treaty be reconsidered,[87] the committee contented itself
by holding the Bolivian request " in its present form "
to be " not in order, because the Assembly of the League
of Nations cannot of itself modify any treaty." [88]
Thus, the real issue was not dealt with, possibly to
avoid an injury to the susceptibilities of the United
States, but more probably because a decision to recommend the reconsideration of a treaty between Chile
and Bolivia would have created a precedent by which
all of the numerous unequal treaties by which most
of the great powers and many of the smaller powers

[87] *Records of the Second Assembly,* Plenary, p. 467.
[88] *Ibid.,* p. 466.

benefit could have been called in question. It is not surprising, therefore, that China's persistent efforts, recently supported by Germany, to persuade the Assembly to fix the procedure by which action shall be taken under Article 19 have proved unavailing.[89]

Thus for the present, Article 19 appears to be virtually a dead letter. This result has not come about because of the unanimity requirement made in the Covenant, for, in spite of the occasional assertions to the effect that unanimity is required for the application of the article, no such decision has been made by the Assembly. Rather, its non-application should be attributed to the Assembly's policy of deliberately avoiding for the time being all discussion of the procedure to be followed in applying the article. This results from the fact that a large proportion of the League members have special interests which they feel would be jeopardized if Article 19 could readily be called into play.

[89] See particularly the remarks of Mr. Chao-Chu Wu (China) in *Records of the Tenth Assembly*, Plenary, p. 99.

CHAPTER VI

MODIFICATIONS ACHIEVED THROUGH FORMAL AMEND-
MENT OF THE COVENANT AND BY TREATY
PROVISIONS

MODIFICATION OF THE UNANIMITY RULE BY FORMAL
AMENDMENT OF THE COVENANT

The League of Nations Covenant has been subjected to few changes through the process of formal amendment. However, the amendment to Article 4 providing that " the Assembly shall fix by a two-thirds majority the rules dealing with the election of the non-permanent Members of the Council, and particularly such regulations as relate to their term of office and the conditions of reeligibility " is of distinct importance in relation to the problem of unanimity, not merely because it adds another instance in which the Assembly may act by less than a unanimous vote, but because of the nature of the regulations which the Assembly has seen fit to adopt in accordance with the provisions of the amendment.

It will be recalled that, when the First Assembly sought to establish regulations pertaining to the selection of the non-permanent members of the Council, certain members expressed the opinion that, inasmuch as such regulations would limit the freedom of choice of the Assembly, the action was beyond the power granted to the Assembly by the Covenant. In deference to the views of these members, the First Assembly gave up the attempt to establish mandatory regulations and contented itself with adopting them in the form of recommendations; recommendations which were renewed from time to time by subsequent Assemblies. However, the Second Assembly, on October 5, 1921, proposed the adoption of the amendment quoted above in order that the Assembly might have power to establish by a two-thirds vote definite rules of an obligatory character governing the selection of the nonpermanent Members of the Council.[1] This amendment came into force July 29, 1926, in accordance with the provisions of Article 26, and on September 15 of the same year the Assembly adopted the regulations for the election, term of office and conditions of reeligibility of the nine non-permanent Members of the Council.[2] Article 3 of those regulations reads as follows:

Notwithstanding the above provisions, the Assembly may at any time by a two-thirds majority decide to proceed, in application of Article 4 of the Covenant, to a new election of all the non-permanent Members of the Council. In this case the Assembly shall determine the rules applicable to the new election.[3]

This regulation, adopted in the autumn following the Council crisis precipitated by Brazil's veto of the resolution granting Germany a permanent Council seat, was proposed by the First Committee and adopted by the Assembly in order to guard against the repetition of such deadlocks. The need for such a rule was called to the attention of the First Committee by Mr. Blythe (Irish Free State) when he expressed his regret that the draft of the regulations proposed by the subcommittee " contained no procedure for allowing the Assembly to withdraw the mandate of a non-permanent Member of the Council." [4] Mr. Blythe felt that the possibility of such a withdrawal would counterbalance the

---

[1] *Records of the Second Assembly*, Plenary, p. 894.

[2] *Records of the Seventh Assembly*, Plenary, p. 80.

[3] *Ibid.*, p. 79.

[4] *Records of the Seventh Assembly*, First Committee, p. 13.

disadvantages which would result from an increase in the number of the non-permanent Council seats. Otherwise, under the new regulations a non-permanent Council Member might pursue an obstructive course for three years.[5]

M. Vogt (Norway) thereupon introduced as an amendment to the regulations before the Committee the proposition which became Article 3 quoted above. In part his defense of it was as follows:

In this paragraph . . . . is offered a clear-cut way, a sharp sword, very probably never to be used and certainly not to be used against a State which, from unselfish motives, pursues a policy of legitimate opposition. But there is a possibility—I do not wish to dwell on the past, I speak hypothetically of the future—there is a possibility that some state may be tempted by the rule of unanimity of Council decisions to take up an attitude of obstruction. There may be temptation, and you increased it the other day by fifty percent. . . . . Hence the necessity of this paragraph. It is a flag hoisted to show the sovereign rights of the Assembly, it is a *mene tekel* written on the wall, an earnest warning—beware. Yes, beware. To give in to obstructive methods would lead to disaster. If a Member of the League would try to press its individual will upon the common will of all nations, it must be met with stern firmness from the very first day—otherwise we shall have to pay the price. . . . .[6]

The proposal of M. Vogt (Norway) was unanimously adopted by the committee after being actively supported by the representatives of Sweden and Denmark and by the representatives of two states having permanent Council seats—Great Britain and Italy. However, M. Loucheur (France), influenced apparently by the fact that the state he represented had allies among the non-permanent Council members, showed little enthusiasm for the proposal. He refrained, however, from active opposition.[7]

[5] *Ibid.*, p. 13.
[6] *Ibid.*, p. 15.
[7] See his remarks in the First Committee. *Records of the Seventh Assembly*, First Committee, p. 17.

When the resolutions were submitted to the Assembly the *rapporteur*, M. Motta (Switzerland), again called attention to the factors which motivated the committee in fixing the terms of Article 3. He spoke in part as follows:

The Assembly—and this is a point I would emphasize—is free at any time to exercise its right to proceed, whenever circumstances call for such action, to a new election of all the non-permanent Members of the Council. Hence no vested right has been created in the seats on the Council. The Assembly remains the sovereign power. It may take away what it has given, but it will only exercise this right by a two-thirds majority and will determine the special rules applicable in this case.

This right reserved by the Assembly . . . . is derived from the general spirit of the Covenant. It does not constitute a menace to anyone—this I would emphasize—it is simply the supreme means whereby the Assembly can intervene to deal with critical situations which admit of no other solution.[8]

The adoption of this regulation, permitting the Assembly by a two-thirds vote to proceed at any time to a new election of all the non-permanent members of the Council, marked a step of far reaching significance in the constitutional development of the League. It virtually arms two-thirds of the Assembly with the power of recall which can be invoked against any nonpermanent Member using its Council seat in a manner not approved by the Assembly. If a non-permanent Member uses its *liberum veto* in a disinterested fashion or if it uses it in order to protect the interests of a considerable group of the smaller League members, recall by the Assembly would appear to be beyond the realm of reasonable probability. On the other hand, should a non-permanent member exercise its veto in such a fashion as to suggest that it is being utilized for purely selfish purposes, the Assembly can forthwith

[8] *Records of the Seventh Assembly*, Plenary, p. 69.

rid the Council of the Member. In all probability the Assembly will not find it necessary to proceed to a utilization of the power. The fact of its existence will no doubt act as a sufficiently potent deterrent to prevent a state occupying a non-permanent seat from deliberately using the unanimity rule to obstruct. Thus it may be said that the unfettered right to obstruct the action of the Council through the unanimity rule for the purpose of protecting one's special interests remains only for those few states which enjoy the favored status accorded to the great powers.

PROVISIONS FOR MAJORITY DECISIONS BY A LEAGUE ORGAN MADE IN INSTRUMENTS OTHER THAN THE COVENANT AND THE TREATIES REFERRED TO IN ARTICLE 5

The tendency toward modification of the unanimity rule can also be observed in the provisions of some of the numerous international instruments which have been drawn up since the drafting of the Covenant and the treaties of which the Covenant forms a part. Strictly speaking, these departures from unanimity do not represent instances in which the League itself has decided to modify the traditional rule, but rather are cases in which certain contracting states have agreed to accept decisions made by a majority vote of a League organ. However, it seems essential that they be dealt with if one is to draw an accurate picture of the extent to which the League functions without observation of the time-honored rule of unanimity. Moreover, the departures from unanimity which will be here enumerated reveal a significant tendency on the part of states members of the League to permit League organs to render decisions without being obli-

gated to achieve unanimity. Some of these decisions
for departures from the unanimity rule are as follows:

1. Part 4 of the Treaty of Lausanne pertaining to
communications and sanitary questions provides that
disputes concerning the Oriental Railways shall be
submitted to the Council for majority decisions. The
Greek and Turkish Governments undertake to carry
out any decision given by such a vote of the Council.[9]

2. Article 4 of the Declaration of the Allied Powers
concerning Albania, November 9, 1921, provides for
decision by the Council on whether intervention seems
advisable to protect the economic integrity and independence of Albania. Should the Council so decide by
majority vote, the Governments shall give new consideration to the question.

3. All decisions concerning the execution of the Second Protocol of the Hungarian Reconstruction Scheme
are to be made by an absolute majority of the Council.[10]

4. The convention between the Principal Allied
Powers and Lithuania concerning Memel provides that
changes in the composition and rights of the harbor
administration and changes in the regulations pertaining to transit through the Memel district may be made
by a majority vote of the Council. However, the representatives of all the Principal Allied Powers must be
on the affirmative side.[11]

5. The Greek Refugees Settlement Scheme of the
League of Nations, drafted September 29, 1923, pro-
vides for taking decisions by a majority vote of the
Council.[12]

6. Decisions concerning disputes arising from the
interpretation of the Bulgarian-Greek financial agree-

[9] Article 107 of the Treaty of Lausanne.
[10] Article 15 of the Treaty of Lausanne.
[11] Section 2, Article 14 and Section 3, Article 4.
[12] Articles 17, 18, 19.

ment of December 9, 1927, are taken by an absolute majority vote of the Council.[13]

7. The Aaland Islands Convention (October 20, 1921) provides that decisions on measures to be taken in case of violation of the demilitarization or neutralization clauses may be taken by a two-thirds majority of the Council.[14]

8. The Treaty of Mutual Guaranty between Germany, Belgium, France, Great Britain and Italy, initialed at Locarno, October 16, 1925, is to remain in force until three months after the Council acting upon the request of one of the signatories decides by a two-thirds vote that the League itself insures sufficient protection to the contracting parties.[15] In case of the violation of the treaty, the contracting parties undertake to act in accordance with the recommendations of the Council provided that they are concurred in by all the members other than the representatives of the parties which have engaged in hostilities.[16]

9. The Geneva Protocol of 1924 provided that the Council, when acting to prevent war under the terms of Articles 7 and 8, could take decisions by a two-thirds majority vote.[17]

10. Article 26 of the agreement drawn up by the Tenth Assembly on Financial Assistance in the Case of War or Threat of War provides that the decision to make a loan to states victims of aggression shall be taken by the Council " by unanimous vote of all the Members present at the meeting, the votes of the representatives of parties to the dispute not being included

[13] Article 9.
[14] Article 7.
[15] Article 8.
[16] Article 4, paragraph 3.
[17] Article 28.

in determining unanimity." [18] All other decisions taken by the Council in respect to this convention are to be by majority vote exclusive of the parties. According to the views expressed in the Third Committee of the Assembly, this meant that unanimity, exclusive of the votes of the parties, would be required only for the decision to make the loan. All decisions concerning such things as the amount, rates of interest, and amortization would be taken by majority vote.[19]

11. In 1931 the Twelfth Assembly drew up and opened for signature and ratification a General Convention to Improve the Means of Preventing War. This convention provides in substance that the Council may, in dealing with such disputes as normally come before it under Article 11, take decisions without the votes of the parties to the dispute counting in determining whether unanimity has been achieved.[20]

If to this list is added those provisions of the Treaties of Versailles, St. Germain, Trianon, and Neuilly, enumerated above,[21] which provide for decision by some majority of the Council, it will become apparent that the cases in which the Council may act by majority, or in which the attempt has been made to allow the Council to act by majority, are rather numerous. It will also appear that many of these departures from unanimity have been made in cases in which the League has been charged with a definitely administrative function. Thus, where it has been recognized that decisions must be taken with alacrity, as, for instance, would be essential in successfully administering the Saar Valley,

[18] *Records of the Tenth Assembly,* Third Committee, p. 60.
[19] *Ibid.,* p. 59.
[20] See particularly Article 7. *Records of the Twelfth Assembly,* Plenary, p. 242.
[21] See above, pp. 39-40.

12

Memel, the minorities question, and the technical questions relating to the extension of financial assistance to the victims of aggression, the majority principle has been approximated. It may be alleged with reason that, in making many of the early decisions to permit the Council to dispense with the customary necessity of unanimity, the powers were motivated by a desire to make it possible to act promptly and vigorously where the affairs of the defeated powers were concerned. They wished to allow them no opportunity to profit because of Council indecision. However, this factor does not explain the more recent tendency to dispense with unanimity in cases in which the Council is called upon to perform administrative functions. That can only be adequately explained as an evidence of the growing recognition that, in dealing with problems of administration, unanimity is both unsatisfactory and unnecessary. It is unsatisfactory because the issues to be settled are often technical in character and effective administration demands that they be settled with promptness and dispatch. It is unnecessary because here political considerations have been reduced to a minimum.

The numerous specific provisions for the exclusion of the interested parties are regarded as being of distinct importance. They indicate an increasing appreciation of the extent to which failure so to provide may jeopardize the possibility of the effective and just settlement of disputes. It also shows a strong determination to create conventions which are workable.

CHAPTER VII

THE EFFECT OF THE UNANIMITY RULE ON THE ASSEMBLY

Resolutions voted by the Assembly may be said to fall roughly into eight more or less distinct classes. These may be described as resolutions of approval, resolutions of guidance, resolutions of request, constitutional resolutions, legislative resolutions, budgetary resolutions, resolutions pertaining to procedural questions, and, finally, resolutions proposing formal amendments to the Covenant. As has been indicated in the preceding pages, the Assembly has held that some types of resolutions do not have to achieve unanimity to order to be adopted by that body. Resolutions pertaining to procedural questions may, of course, be adopted by majority vote. As we have seen, matters of procedure have been interpreted to include such things as the election of the non-permanent members of the Council and decisions to set up investigating committees, as well as matters which would clearly be described under this heading, such as fixing the order of business and electing the Assembly officers. Moreover, it does not seem unreasonable to expect that in the next few years the requesting of advisory opinions from the World Court will be definitely included in this category. Resolutions of amendment, as has been pointed out above, are not considered to be decisions within the meaning of Article 5 and, therefore, unanimity is not required. Budgetary resolutions must be adopted by unanimous vote in the plenary session but, as has been indicated above, it has become the practice of the Assembly for the minority to give way to the majority when questions of this nature are under consideration. Finally, resolutions of guidance, of request, and of approval can readily be changed into recommendations requiring only a majority vote if it becomes apparent that unanimity can not be achieved in the Assembly. For example, a resolution requesting the Council to appoint an investigating committee may be changed into a resolution recommending that the Council appoint an investigating committee. Likewise resolutions of approval of the work of some League organ or of guidance for some League organ may be changed into resolutions recommending that a certain course of action be continued or adopted. It is submitted that resolutions which embody such recommendations and which receive the approval of a large majority of the Assembly members, including the votes of all the great powers, will possess virtually the same force as resolutions receiving the unanimous approval of the Assembly.

There remain, therefore, but two classes of Assembly resolutions for which it has been held that unanimity is essential, or for which custom does not require that the minority give way to the majority; namely, constitutional resolutions and legislative resolutions. The former purport to give authoritative interpretations to the articles of the Covenant, while the latter inaugurate international conventions which, after signature and accession thereto, become legally binding obligations for the ratifying states. Even here the rigor of the unanimity rule has been greatly reduced by the extra-legal practice of taking decisions in the committees by majority vote, by the practice of counting abstentions as absences, and by the failure of the Assembly to fix a quorum requirement for transacting business. When to this it is added that there exists in the Assembly a desire to agree, and that quite naturally no member wishes to find himself a minority of one obstructing the adoption of a resolution, it must become apparent that the unanimity rule does not constitute such a serious obstacle to the successful functioning of the Assembly as one would be led to conclude from a casual reading of the Covenant. However, the attempt will here be made to demonstrate with some degree of precision the extent to which the Assembly has been obstructed through the existence of the *liberum veto*.

As might be expected, the cases in which propositions having received the affirmative vote of a majority of the Assembly are declared defeated because of failure to achieve unanimity are not numerous. There have been only two such instances. The first occurred during the sessions of the Second Assembly. The proposition failing of adoption involved an interpretation of Article 18 of the Covenant. As some doubt existed as to the scope of this article, the First Committee had proposed that the following amendment be added to it:

It shall not be obligatory to submit for registration instruments of a purely technical or administrative nature which have no bearing on political international relations, nor instruments which consist merely of technical regulations defining, without in any way modifying, an instrument already registered, or which are only designed to enable such an instrument to be carried into effect.[1]

When this amendment was reported to the Assembly proper, several members, feeling that its adoption might endanger the whole principle of Article 18, expressed the opinion that it would be better to postpone consideration until a later date. Mr. Balfour (British Empire) thereupon introduced two resolutions, one providing for the postponement and the

[1] *Records of the Second Assembly,* Plenary, p. 702.

other that it be understood that "in the meantime
Members of the League are at liberty to interpret their
obligations under Article 18 in conformity with the
proposed amendment." [2] The first Balfour resolution
received unanimous approval, while the second received
twenty-eight affirmative votes and five negative, the
negative votes apparently being cast by five of the
smaller powers.[3] Both resolutions were declared by
the President, M. Van Karnebeek (Netherlands),
to have been adopted, the latter because it was at first
considered to be a recommendation requiring only a
majority vote. However, the President was obliged to
reverse his holding on Balfour's second resolution, as
it was called to his attention by M. Restrepo (Colombia) that the proposition was in fact a resolution purporting to interpret the Covenant rather than one
embodying a simple recommendation.[4] The constitutional resolution was therefore declared to have been
"not accepted," care thus being taken to make it clear
that the Assembly had not rejected the principle involved in the resolution in favor of the contrary view.[5]

The Fourth Assembly supplies the second instance
of a resolution failing to be adopted although having a majority vote cast for it. The proposition in
question was the famous Canadian resolution interpreting Article 10 of the Covenant. In the First Assembly

[2] *Ibid.*, p. 851.

[3] *Ibid.*, p. 852. The vote was in this case taken by the delegates
rising in their seats. Hence, no record exists to show which states cast
affirmative and which negative votes. However, if one judges from
the context of the debates it appears exceedingly probable that the
negative votes were cast by five small states. Only the delegates of
Colombia, South Africa, Switzerland, and the Serb-Croat-Slovene
State spoke against the resolution.

[4] *Records of the Second Assembly*, Plenary, p. 895.

[5] *Ibid.*, p. 895.

the Canadian delegation had suggested the removal of Article 10 from the Covenant and in the Second and Third Assemblies they had sponsored amendments to the article, only to have consideration on each occasion postponed. In the Fourth Assembly they again submitted the amendment but, at the suggestion of the First Committee, changed it into an interpretative resolution. Two factors appear to have been responsible for this change. In the first place, many delegates were of the opinion that the end sought by Canada could be better accomplished by a resolution setting forth the Assembly's views on the meaning of Article 10 than by making a change in the wording of the article. In the second place, the interpretative resolution appeared to be more feasible than an amendment, inasmuch as none of the amendments proposed by the Second Assembly had as yet been ratified by enough states to come into effect in accordance with the provisions of Article 26. The text of the resolution submitted was as follows:

The Assembly, desirous of defining the scope of the obligations contained in Article 10 of the Covenant so far as the points raised by the delegation of Canada, adopts the following resolution:

It is in conformity with the spirit of Article 10 that, in the event of the Council considering it to be its duty to recommend the application of military measures in consequence of an aggression or danger or threat of aggression, the Council shall be bound to take account, more particularly of the geographical situation and of the special conditions of each State.

It is for the constitutional authorities of each Member to decide, in reference to the obligation of preserving the independence and the integrity of the territory of Members, in what degree the Member is bound to assume the execution of this obligation by employment of its military forces.

The recommendation made by the Council shall be regarded as being of the highest importance, and shall be taken into consideration by all the Members of the League with the desire to execute their engagements in good faith.[6]

---

[6] *Records of the Fourth Assembly,* Plenary, p. 86.

When the resolution was put to a vote it received twenty-nine affirmative votes, one negative (Persia) and twenty-two were reported as absent or abstaining.[7] All those states having permanent Council representation voted in favor of the resolution. The President, M. Peraza (Cuba) announced that in accordance with a precedent which arose in a similar case he was unable to declare the resolution rejected but rather he had to declare the proposal not adopted.[8]

The results of the votes on these two resolutions do not appear to entail serious consequences for the League. It does not appear that the majority has been seriously obstructed in guiding the League in the paths it has desired. For even though the two resolutions were declared " not adopted " it should be remembered that in both instances the presiding officer took occasion to point out that the resolutions could not be declared to have been defeated. Can it be doubted that in reality Article 18 and Article 10 are interpreted in accordance with the resolutions which failed to attain the formal approval of the Assembly? Is not a pronouncement on the meaning of the Covenant made by the large majority of Members, including all of the powers occupying permanent Council seats, virtually as authoritative as one in which all Members concur?

---

[7] *Ibid.*, p. 87. It is occasionally asserted that the abstention of twenty-two states indicates that that number supported the position of Persia. However, closer investigation will show that of the twenty-two the representatives of nine were physically absent when the vote was taken (Argentine, Bolivia, Colombia, Guatemala, Honduras, Nicaragua, Paraguay, Peru and the Serb-Croat-Slovene State). Thirteen states were present but abstained from voting (Albania, Costa Rica, Czechoslovakia, Esthonia, Finland, Haiti, Latvia, Liberia, Lithuania, Panama, Poland, Siam and Venezuela).

[8] *Records of the Fourth Assembly*, Plenary, p. 87.

To the writer it would so appear. Therefore, it seems
that, although the negative vote of Persia, supported
by the thirteen abstaining states, may be said to have
blocked the formal adoption by the Assembly of a resolution interpreting Article 10, it does not appear that
they blocked the interpretation of Article 10. Likewise in the case of Article 18, the five negative votes
may be said to have prevented the adoption of the
resolution of interpretation, but the very fact that
twenty-eight other states, including all the Great
Powers, went on record favoring that interpretation
makes it highly probably that in the actual practice of
states the article will be accorded that meaning. It
does not, therefore, appear that the unanimity rule
has presented an insurmountable obstacle to the Assembly when that body has been called upon to deal with
resolutions of constitutional interpretation.

However, the obstruction resulting from the existence of the *liberum veto* cannot be measured solely by
a consideration of those cases in which propositions
have failed of adoption because some negative votes
have been cast. It is necessary that one look behind the
formal votes in the Assembly to discover to what extent
resolutions desired by a majority have been " watered
down " in order that they may receive the favorable
votes of all and, perhaps, to discover cases in which the
sponsors of propositions have withdrawn them rather
than allow them to go down to defeat because a small
minority is unwilling to acquiesce in their adoption.
As one might expect, it is only by such a process that
the obstructive nature of the unanimity rule in the
Assembly can be measured with any degree of accu-
racy. Therefore, each case in which a majority of the
Assembly has felt obliged to modify seriously or to
withdraw a proposed resolution because of the irrecon-

cilable opposition of a minority will be given consideration. It is believed that as a result of such a survey it
will be possible to draw more definite conclusions in
regard to the effect of the unanimity rule in the Assembly, as well as to come to certain conclusions in respect
to the rôle played by the large and by the small states
in the game of utilizing the provisions of Article 5,
paragraph 1, to protect special interests.

During the course of the meetings of the First Assembly, two important propositions, both clearly desired
by a majority, were sacrificed in deference to the principle of unanimity. Both pertained to the Statute of the
World Court. The plan for the Court had been drawn
up and unanimously adopted by a Committee of Jurists
meeting at the Hague. It was referred by that body to
the Council, where one change of importance, the strik-
ing out of the compulsory jurisdiction clause, was made
before that body passed it on to the Assembly. The
Statute was referred by the Assembly to its Third Committee for study and report. The discussion in that body
centered in the main around two questions; namely,
whether the compulsory jurisdiction clause should be
reinserted and whether the Assembly by its own pronouncement had sufficient power to declare the Court
to be in existence.

A consideration of the debates which took place in
the Third Committee and in the Plenary Session leaves
no doubt concerning the overwhelming character of
the majority which desired the compulsory jurisdiction
clause to be contained in the Statute. However, this
majority was made up for the most part of representatives of the smaller states. M. Lafontaine (Belgium)
may be said to have led the fight for the return of the
clause to the Statute and his most active support came
chiefly from among the representatives of the small

states, such as M. Pueyrredon of Argentine, M. Arias of Panama, M. Costa of Portugal, M. Urriatia of Colombia, and M. Fernandes of Brazil. Only the delegates of the British Empire and France openly opposed,[9] although Lord Robert Cecil (South Africa), M. Loder (Netherlands), and M. Hagerup (Norway) urged that the majority " calculate the limits of the possible " and compromise.[10] However, in order that unanimity might be obtained, the attempt to establish compulsory jurisdiction was given up and the optional clause inserted as a substitute.[11] That the majority felt themselves thwarted by the minority is clearly indicated by the following words of M. Lafontaine (Belgium) :

> The nations had another hope; namely, that recourse to international justice would be compulsory for all disputes. In this case also a minority of the delegations has once more paralysed the will of the majority. I will not recapitulate the explanations which have been given you by the speakers who preceded me. I will only mention two of the arguments which were advanced against us.
>
> I was astonished to hear those who once defended the principle of compulsory arbitration utter the words " vital interests." I heard proclaimed the absolute sovereignty of States. We were told that only nations themselves were judges of their vital interests and that to recognize the right of a State to arraign another was a grave encroachment upon the sovereignty of States. This is not the moment to discuss these principles again. They are condemned by the general opinion of the world.
>
> When I heard these arguments it seemed to me that a shadow haunted the room in which we sat, the shadow of a broad-shouldered cavalryman, of a tall Junker, who was the cause of our failure at the Hague in 1907.[12]

---

[9] See particularly the remarks of M. Bourgeois (France) and Mr. Balfour (British Empire) in *Records of the First Assembly,* Plenary, pp. 493 and 487, respectively.

[10] *Ibid.,* p. 445.

[11] Article 36, Statute of the World Court.

[12] *Records of the First Assembly,* Plenary, p. 447.

In respect to the second point at issue, namely, whether it was essential that the Statute be first adopted by unanimous vote of the Assembly and then ratified by the States, as had been the customary procedure for the adoption of conventions, or whether a unanimous vote by the Assembly might suffice of itself for establishing the Court, the majority was again obliged to give way to the minority. M. Politis (Greece)[13] and M. Negulesco (Roumania)[14] insisted that action by the Assembly was nothing but a stage in the preparation of the final plan to be submitted to the governments for ratification, and that under no circumstances could they see ratification dispensed with. Inasmuch as these two members refused to give way to the will of the great majority, ratification could not be dispensed with and consequently the League lost the opportunity to take a step which would have done much toward marking it out as a corporate entity possessing a will quite separate and distinct from that of the individual states forming the League. The words of M. Lafontaine (Belgium) again indicate that the failure to take this forward step may rightly be attributed to a minority:

Article 14 of the Covenant provides that the scheme for the establishment of the Court should be submitted to the Members of the League. With a little daring it was possible to interpret these words as the Council has done, and to decide to submit the draft statute not to the Members of the League but to the Assembly.

But the daring that was applauded a few weeks ago has waned, and the rule of unanimity will oblige us and the majority of the Assembly to accept the will of a few. We dreamed of the moment when the Supreme Court might enter in state into the hall of judgment and thenceforward enunciate there by unanimous consent the principles of law. But our Court will enter by the side door of a

---

13 *Ibid.*, p. 482.
14 *Ibid.*, p. 453.

succession of ratifications and assents. It might have been created, to all intents and purposes, this very day. It might have been the magnificent result of a unanimous impulse of justice which would have satisfied the world. It is right that the world should know that decisive action on our part is only prevented by the opposition of a few.[15]

However, this loss was in part compensated for. By way of compromise an important precedent was established. Acting upon the suggestion of M. Hagerup (Norway), the Assembly decided that, after the Statute had been approved by a unanimous vote of the Assembly, it should be submitted to the Governments in the form of a Protocol. Provision was made to the effect that when this Protocol should be ratified by a majority of the Members of the League the Court should be declared to be in existence. Thus, the First Assembly established the practice of regarding a convention as acceptable after it has received a limited number of ratifications. No state, of course, which has not ratified is bound by such a convention, but the convention is permitted to come into force between the ratifying parties, with a consequent indirect influence upon those governments which have not ratified. This, it is believed, is the first case in which the League deliberately dispensed with the necessity of unanimity where ratifications are concerned.

The Seventh Assembly presents an excellent example of a resolution which might have been strong being " watered down " to a weak expression of hope in order that all might vote for it. This resolution, relating to the International Economic Conference, as finally adopted by the Assembly read as follows:

The Assembly notes that the Council has given effect to its decision of December 15, 1925, by constituting a Preparatory Committee for the International Economic Conference.

---

[15] *Ibid.*, p. 446.

It realizes that the general economic situation of the world calls more imperiously than ever for an effort towards international co-operation and makes it yet more necessary that the Economic Conference should be held.

The Assembly therefore hopes that the Committee will actively push forward its work, so as to enable the Economic Conference to be convened as soon as possible.[16]

Had the majority of the members of the Second Committee had their way, the resolution would have urged that the Council convene the conference within the year, that it be made up of experts not instructed by the appointing governments, and that it be authorized to deal with such questions as tariff barriers.[17] However, the representative of France, M. Loucheur, opposed at every turn the attempts of the majority of small states, supported in part by the representative of the British Empire, to induce the committee to recommend the adoption of such a resolution.[18] To be sure, such a resolution could have been passed in the form of a recommendation to the Council by a majority vote of the Assembly without the concurrence of France, but it would have carried little weight. It no doubt seemed more expedient for the majority to allow the resolution to be modified so that all could vote for it. However, before the resolution was put to a vote in the plenary session it was roundly condemned by M. Adelsward (Sweden), who had led the struggle in the committee for a resolution of stronger character.[19]

[16] *Records of the Seventh Assembly*, Plenary, p. 92.

[17] See particularly the remarks of M. Di Pauli (Austria), *Records of the Seventh Assembly*, Second Committee, p. 35, and those of M. Adelsward (Sweden), *ibid.*, p. 37.

[18] *Ibid.*, pp. 35, 41.

[19] *Records of the Seventh Assembly*, Plenary, p. 91.

On another occasion the Seventh Assembly was obliged to postpone consideration of a resolution, the adoption of which had been recommended by the First Committee, because of the opposition of France and Czechoslovakia. The proposition, formulated by the First Committee upon the initiative of the British delegation, had for its goal an interpretation of the Preamble and Articles 3 and 4 of the Covenant. It read as follows:

The Assembly, recognizes that the League of Nations should avoid dissipating its activity upon subjects which might divert it from its lofty mission of promoting the peace of the world and facilitating co-operation between nations for the peaceful progress of mankind;

Recommends that each body forming part of the League, before taking into consideration any proposal submitted to it, should satisfy itself that the proposal is in accordance with the objects of the League as indicated by the Covenant and possess real importance from the point of view of the attainment of those objects;

Decides that in the case of doubt, and if so requested by a member of the body, the question shall be submitted to the Council, in the interval between the sessions of the Assembly, and, during those sessions, to the Committee appointed by the Assembly for legal and constitutional questions.

The present resolution shall be brought by the Secretary-General to the knowledge of the various bodies forming part of the League.[20]

The Delegates of France and Czechoslovakia understood this resolution to be an attempt to provide machinery for drawing a line between international questions and domestic questions, in short, between questions with which the League could and those with which it could not deal. Evidently they preferred that such machinery should not exist. According to M. Barthélemy (France) they were motivated by the fear that a " rigid or restrictive legal definition might one day hamper the League in the performance of its duties." [21]

20 *Ibid.*, p. 413.
21 *Ibid.*, p. 125.

M. Motta (Switzerland), Chairman of the First Committee, said that, in view of the opposition which existed to the adoption of the resolution, "postponement is clearly advisable." [22] The resolution was not, therefore, put to a vote.

The Eleventh Assembly presents an example of a minority obliging the majority to substitute a resolution of a weak and almost meaningless character for one which undoubtedly pointed in the direction of strong, effective action by the League in dealing with the problem of slavery.

By a resolution passed by the Tenth Assembly, the League had instructed the Secretary-General to collect from the Member States and also from non-Member States parties to the Slavery Convention (September 25, 1926) all possible information on the present situation in respect to slavery. This information was to be transmitted by the Secretary-General to the Assembly. However, the information collected was admittedly inadequate chiefly because many of the governments concerned did not send in to the Secretary-General the information that they had on hand. Therefore, in order that the League might be able to deal more effectively with the problem of slavery, the British delegation submitted to the Sixth Committee of the Eleventh Assembly a proposal to create a permanent slavery commission and an international slavery office somewhat comparable to the machinery existing for dealing with the problem of mandates.

Although the British proposal was warmly supported in the Sixth Committee by the delegates of a majority of the Members, it was actively opposed by the representatives of Abyssinia, Belgium, France,

[22] *Ibid.*, p. 127.

Liberia, Netherlands, and Portugal—the very states which would be affected by the control that the British resolution proposed to expedite. The representatives of these states raised three principal objections to the creation of the commission. In the first place, if it confined itself merely to the collection of information it was declared that it would merely duplicate a function being performed by the Secretariat. Secondly, if it were given supervisory powers it would trample upon the sovereignty and independence of states. The position of the Permanent Mandates Commission was not considered comparable because the formation of that body had been authorized by the peace treaties. Finally, whatever its nature, it would add an additional burden to the League budget.[23]

Because of the opposition of this group, the resolution sponsored by the British delegation had to be withdrawn. In its place the following was substituted by the Sixth Committee:

The Assembly, having taken note of the communications received from a large number of Governments in pursuance of the resolution of the Tenth Assembly;

Observing that the number of ratifications of the Convention of September 25, 1926, has risen in one year from 29 to 34, but that the information furnished by the States Members of the League has not so far been such as to give an accurate idea of the present general situation in regard to slavery;

Desiring, however, to wait until next year for the results of the procedure now in force;

Postpones, provisionally, consideration of any possible changes in the procedure; and

Invites the States Members of the League and States non-Members to amplify the information they have already given by furnishing

<hr>

[23] See particularly the remarks of M. Sottile (Liberia), *Records of the Eleventh Assembly*, Sixth Committee, p. 59; M. Francois-Poncet (France), *ibid.*, p. 62; Count Garcia (Portugal), *ibid.*, p. 67; and Count Bonin-Longare (Italy), *ibid.*, p. 73.

all such particulars as may assist the Assembly to form an idea, not only of the conditions that prevail in their own territories, but of the present general position in regard to slavery.[24]

This resolution was adopted by unanimous vote, the British Empire abstaining.[25] As Viscount Cecil put it, his delegation found it impossible to vote for " this somewhat inconclusive decision although it does not think it necessary to vote against it." [26]

Finally, in the Twelfth Assembly a resolution less far-reaching than the majority desired was reported to the Assembly and adopted because of the opposition of a few to the more drastic proposal desired. The resolution in question pertained to a truce in armaments prior to and during the meeting of the World Disarmament Conference. In the Third Committee the delegates of Denmark, Norway, the Netherlands, Sweden, and Switzerland introduced a resolution calling upon the Assembly to

request the Council to urge the Governments convened to the said Conference to show their firm determination to support the efforts to ensure peace and reestablish mutual confidence by abstaining, pending the result of the Conference, from any measure leading to an increase in the present level of their armaments.[27]

General de Marinis (Italy) believed this draft resolution to be entirely inadequate. In its place he proposed to substitute a resolution which would not only call for an armanent truce but would provide for its practical application. He proposed that the states be invited to agree to such things as not to increase their military budgets, not to lay down any new warships, and not to construct any new military aircraft.[28]

[24] *Records of the Eleventh Assembly,* Plenary, p. 154.
[25] *Ibid.,* p. 156.
[26] *Ibid.,* p. 155.
[27] *Records of the Twelfth Assembly,* Third Committee, p. 30.
[28] *Ibid.,* p. 33.

In the Third Committee the plan of the Italian delegation received the active support of the representatives of seventeen states, including the British Empire and Germany.[29] It was opposed only by the delegates of four states—M. Massigli (France), M. Sato (Japan), M. Sokal (Poland) and M. Fotitch (Jugoslavia). M. Massigli (France) declared that the Italian proposal "was entirely to the benefit of one of the parties concerned,"[30] a charge which General de Marinis (Italy) bitterly denied.[31] M. Sokal (Poland), following the lead of France, declared that the plan was unnecessary because the economic and financial crisis made it impossible to increase armaments.[32] M. Sato (Japan) found the plan impractical because "exact information would be required as to the present level of armaments."[33] In the words of M. Motta (Switzerland) since "the more definite proposal of the Italian delegation had no prospect of being unanimously adopted there was nothing to do but to accept the proposal of the five powers."[34] Therefore, in order that unanimity might be achieved in the Assembly, the Third Committee recommended in substance the adoption of the resolution suggested by the five powers. They did add the provision that the Council be requested "to ask the Governments to state before November 1, 1931, whether they are prepared for a period of one year as from this date to accept this truce in armaments." The resolution was subsequently adopted by unanimous vote of the Assembly.[35]

[29] *Ibid.*, pp. 33-55.
[30] *Ibid.*, p. 43.
[31] *Ibid.*, p. 46.
[32] *Ibid.*, p. 41.
[33] *Ibid.*, p. 40.
[34] *Ibid.*, p. 45.
[35] *Records of the Twelfth Assembly,* Plenary, p. 161.

We may say, therefore, that on six occasions the will of the majority of the Assembly has been definitely thwarted by that of the minority without a vote having been resorted to. The First Assembly was prevented from including a provision for compulsory jurisdiction in the World Court Statute by the opposition of France and the British Empire, and they were unable to dispense with ratification because of the opposition to the move on the part of Greece and Roumania. The majority of the members of the Seventh Assembly found themselves unable, because of the opposition of France, to follow their inclinations and urge that the Council fix a definite date for the assembling of the Economic Conference, that the Council request the Governments to name uninstructed delegates, and that the Council provide that the agenda include such questions as tariff barriers. Likewise the Seventh Assembly was obliged to postpone consideration of a resolution interpretive of the Preamble and Articles 3 and 4 of the Covenant because of opposition coming from France and her ally, Czechoslovakia. The Eleventh Assembly was unable to propose the creation of a Permanent Slavery Commission because of the opposition of France and Italy and five other powers, all of which would have been directly affected by the proposed commission. Finally, in the Twelfth Assembly, Japan and France, supported by two of France's allies, blocked the attempt of the majority to substitute undertakings of a definite character for the rather vague wording of the request that there be an armaments truce.

It has no doubt been observed that, in five of the six cases in which the majority of the Assembly has been blocked by a minority, one or more of the great powers has been included in that minority. Indeed, no small power or combination of small powers has been successful in an attempt to prevent the taking of a decision desired by the majority of the Assembly since the first year of the League's existence, unless Persia's veto of the resolution interpretive of Article 10 be counted. The survey of the practice of the Assembly indicates that small powers are not by themselves permitted to hinder the functioning of that body in spite of the provisions of Article 5. Either they are persuaded to abstain or the resolutions to which they are opposed are passed in the form of recommendations not requiring absolute unanimity. It is not meant to imply that the views of the delegates of the smaller states are of no importance, or that they are treated as such in the Assembly. On the contrary, many of the delegates of the smaller powers, because of their capabilities and long experience in the Assembly, have great influence there. The position that some of them take upon the issues raised in the Assembly may have great bearing upon world opinion, a factor which can not be ignored by the representatives of the great powers. Nevertheless, the fact remains that it is only the representatives of the great powers who can stand out persistently in the face of a hostile Assembly majority and refuse to give way. The representatives of the small states know that, should the delegation of a single small state or the delegations of a few small states attempt to block the majority by use of the unanimity rule in the Assembly, the majority will resort to one of the several methods by which that rule can be successfully circumvented.[36]

[36] The threats of representatives of the smaller powers to exercise the *liberum veto* are more numerous than the cases in which it has actually been used. See particularly the remarks of M. Edwards (Chile), *Records of the Second Assembly,* Plenary, p. 467; M. Osusky

In spite of the number of cases that have been cited
here in which the minority has persisted in its opposition to the will of the majority to such an extent
that propositions have had to be seriously modified
or abandoned altogether, a reading of the debates
which have taken place in the plenary sessions of the
Assembly and particularly in the committees can not
fail to convince one that normally, when differences of
opinion arise, small minorities give way to majorities.
No delegation enjoys being a minority of one or even
a part of a somewhat larger minority which has incurred the disfavor that is heaped upon those who
obstruct the smooth functioning of the League machinery. The very fact that the delegations are brought
together in one hall tends to foster a spirit of loyalty
and cooperation which has the effect of inducing delegations finding themselves in opposition to stand aside
whenever possible to allow decisions desired by the
great majority to be taken. It results that small minorities ordinarily make no attempt to block the course
of the majority except in special circumstances in which
strong political motives are at work.

Perhaps the strongest proof that can be given of
the truth of these assertions is to call attention once
more to the number of decisions taken by majority
vote in the committees, the resolutions then being
adopted without change by the unanimous vote of the
Assembly. Normally the minority, which may occasionally include a Member occupying a permanent
Council seat, expresses its disapproval of the resolution by abstention.[37] On other occasions, however, it

(Czechoslovakia), *Records of the Eighth Assembly,* Fourth Committee, p. 63; and of the Earl of Lytton (India), *Records of the
Ninth Assembly,* Plenary, p. 188.

[37] See, for example, *Records of the Eleventh Assembly,* Plenary,
p. 163.

is necessary that the taking of votes be delayed so that the minority can be persuaded by means of informal conferences to give way to the majority.[38] On such occasions slight concessions are sometimes made to the minority, a practice which, of course, militates to some extent against the vigor, meaning, and scope of Assembly resolutions.

[38] See *Records of the First Assembly*, Plenary, p. 299; *ibid.*, p. 336.

CHAPTER VIII

THE EFFECT OF THE UNANIMITY RULE ON THE COUNCIL

The terms of the Covenant provide fewer exceptions to the general rule of unanimity for the Council than for the Assembly. Several articles specify, for example, that an action may be taken by a majority vote of the Assembly following a unanimous vote of the Council.[1] Provisions of this character may be explained, of course, as the result of a desire to allow the Great Powers to protect their interests, and as the result of a belief that unanimity would be less difficult to achieve in a body as small as the original Council than in a body the size of the Assembly.

However, in contrast to these Covenant provisions, the treaties referred to in Article 5 of the Covenant, and many of the treaties entered into by League members after the League had been functioning for some time, provide numerous and important exceptions to the unanimity rule in the Council.[2] Moreover, the Council, like the Assembly, has made the most of such exceptions to the general rule of unanimity as are provided for in the Covenant; and, on occasion, it has proved to be rather adept in discovering gaps in the rule which can scarcely have occurred to those persons responsible for the drafting of the Covenant.

The most important of the specific exceptions to the unanimity rule provided for in the Covenant is, no

---

[1] Articles 4, 6, and 26, for example.
[2] For a list of these, see above, pp. 39-40 and 162-165.

doubt, the provision of Article 5, paragraph 2, which permits the Council, as well as the Assembly, to determine all questions of a procedural character by majority vote. As has been indicated above, the Council has interpreted this provision rather broadly, holding, for example, that it may set up commissions of inquiry by majority vote. Moreover, it seems highly probable that the clause will ultimately be interpreted to allow the requesting of advisory opinions from the World Court by a majority vote of either the Council or the Assembly. Also, as was pointed out above, the Council has on occasion ruled that the votes of parties to a dispute or parties against whom a judgment is to be executed may be excluded, even when the Council is acting under the terms of articles which make no specific statement to this effect. Although no definite statement of the course which the League will pursue in the future can, of course, be made, it seems quite possible that the League may yet decide to exclude the votes of the interested parties in all cases in which the Council or the Assembly is acting in a judicial capacity. This practice, even though not as yet followed consistently, has served to reduce the rigor of the unanimity rule in the Council.

It should also be noted that the Council has made the achievement of unanimity less difficult than it would otherwise be by adopting the Assembly practice of counting those members who abstain from voting as absent, rather than insisting that all those physically present must cast affirmative votes in order that a resolution be deemed to have achieved unanimity. Inasmuch as the Council rules of procedure provide that a majority constitutes a quorum, this ruling forms a modification of real importance to the unanimity rule.

The Council, however, has never seen fit to adopt
that most effective Assembly device for escaping the
necessity of unanimity; namely, the use of the "recommendation." Logically, the Council as well as the
Assembly might hold that decisions which impose no
direct obligation upon the member states are not
"decisions" within the meaning of Article 5 of the
Covenant. If that line of reasoning can hold in the
Assembly, it is difficult to see why it could not in the
Council. However, in 1921, the Council Committee
on Amendments to the Covenant as well as the First
Committee of the Second Assembly went definitely
upon record as opposed to the extension of this practice to the Council, justifying this difference between the practice of the two bodies by stating that
the maintenance of the unanimity rule was essential
to the prestige of the Council, "the essentially active
organ of the League," and by declaring that experience indicated that unanimity was not difficult to
secure in a body as small as the Council.[3] Although
this position was taken before the Council had been
enlarged to its present size and before many of the
provisions for majority decision by the Council had
been made by treaties between League members, the
Council has not as yet felt obliged to change its stand
upon this matter.

It has been noted that the achievement of unanimity
in the Assembly has been made less difficult than it
otherwise would be by the practice, quite generally
adhered to, of giving unanimous approval in the plenary meetings to resolutions adopted by large majorities in the committees. To a certain limited extent this
practice has its counterpart in the Council. Although

[3] See above, pp. 107-108.

the Council does not employ a committee system comparable to that of the Assembly, it is the practice of that body to designate from among its own membership a *rapporteur* upon each type of question that comes before it. These individuals, working in cooperation with the Secretariat, prepare reports and resolutions to be placed before the Council. Frequently, such resolutions are discussed informally, or, perhaps, even in the " Council of Twelve," and agreement upon them is reached prior to the formal meeting of the Council. This practice may, of course, result in compromises which weaken the Council resolutions. It has the merit, however, of making some agreement possible and, on occasion, it is useful in allowing the great majority of the Council to present a united front against the member who otherwise might feel sufficiently bold to obstruct.

However, in spite of the numerous loopholes in the unanimity rule which have been discovered by the Council, that body has on several occasions been delayed, obstructed, and even defeated through the use of the *liberum veto* or the threat of its use by one or more of the Council members. This appears to have occurred first in 1921, when Brazil prevented Spain from pressing her claim for a permanent Council seat by allowing it to be known that she would veto the proposition.[4] Inasmuch as Article 4, paragraph 2, of the Covenant provides that the number of permanent Council members can be increased only by a unanimous vote of the Council approved by a majority of the Assembly, a permanent seat could not be provided for Spain so long as Brazil remained on the Council and

---

[4] *Committee on the Composition of the Council:* Report on the Work of the First Session, p. 12. (League Doc. C. 299. M. 139. 1926 V.)

so long as she maintained her opposition to the proposal. The proposal for the creation of a permanent seat for Spain was, therefore, temporarily dropped, only to come up in a more acute form in 1926.

On at least three occasions the Council has been prevented by the opposition of a single state from appealing to the World Court for an advisory opinion upon the legal issues involved in the dispute before it. It may be said that upon each of these occasions the Council has been prevented from adopting the procedure which it has felt to be best suited for bringing about a satisfactory settlement to the dispute, being obliged, as a consequence, to turn to some other procedure in which the large majority of the Council members have had less faith.

In 1923, a prompt settlement of the Hungarian Optants dispute between Roumania and Hungary, submitted to the Council by Hungary under Article 11, paragraph 2, of the Covenant, was prevented through use of the veto by Roumania. M. Adatci (Japan), *rapporteur*, first suggested that the most satisfactory method of reaching a solution in this case would be for " the parties themselves to submit the dispute to the legal authority set up in accordance with the Covenant of the League of Nations: the Permanent Court of International Justice." [5] M. Lukacs (Hungary) announced the willingness of his country to accept this procedure.[6] M. Titulesco (Roumania), however, declared that since the two countries were not divided upon a question of law alone, he found himself unable to accept on behalf of his government the proposition of M. Adatci.[7] M. Adatci thereupon proposed that

[5] *O. J.*, 1923, p. 605.
[6] *Ibid.*, p. 605.
[7] *Ibid.*, p. 606.

the Council should ask for an advisory opinion from the World Court, " it being understood that the Council's freedom of decision would be in no way limited." [8] To this second proposal of the *rapporteur*, M. Lukacs (Hungary) again assented, adding that in this case a unanimous vote would not be required inasmuch as it was a matter of procedure.[9] However, M. Titulesco (Roumania) again opposed, and since the Council was not at the time disposed to accept M. Lukacs' version of the vote required for requesting an advisory opinion from the World Court, the Council was obliged to postpone consideration.[10] However, it is important to note that up to the present time both the Council and the Assembly have carefully avoided a decision to the effect that unanimity is *required* for the requesting of an opinion.

In 1928, Roumania again through use of the veto prevented the Hungarian Optants dispute from going before the World Court for an advisory opinion.[11] A year before, the negative vote of Germany alone had prevented the Council from acting favorably upon Greece's request that the Court be called upon for an advisory opinion in the " Salamis " case.[12]

In 1926, because of the existence of the unanimity rule in the Council, the League found itself completely blocked in the plan to admit Germany to the League with permanent Council membership in accordance with the terms of the agreement reached at Locarno. Soon after the terms of the agreement became known, Spain and Brazil, both occupying temporary Council

[8] *Ibid.,* p. 608.
[9] *Ibid.,* p. 608.
[10] *Ibid.,* p. 609.
[11] *O. J.,* 1928, p. 439.
[12] *O. J.,* 1927, p. 1475.

seats, intimated that it was their intention to use their veto power in the Council to block the proposed admission of Germany as a permanent Council member unless they, too, were accorded such a status.[13] Shortly after the position of Spain and Brazil became known, came the announcement that Poland also would demand a permanent seat. The situation was made more difficult by the knowledge that Poland was being backed in her position by France and that Spain had a pledge of British support, dating from the time at which her claim for such a position had been advanced in 1921. The announcement of Poland's claim was followed by similar claims by Czechoslovakia, China, and Persia. The German government thereupon let it be known that unless Germany received a permanent Council seat without similar awards being made to other states she would not consent to enter the League. It was in the face of this situation that the Council on February 12, 1926, called the special session of the Assembly to meet March 8, 1926, for the purpose of dealing with the request of Germany for admission to the League and deciding upon " the proposals which might be made by the Council in application of Article 4 of the Covenant." [14]

Shortly before the Assembly was to have convened in its first special session, Sweden, an occupant of a non-permanent Council seat, announced that she would vote against a permanent seat for Poland, should it be proposed in the Council to accord Poland such a status.

---

[13] On the Council deadlock of 1926 compare J. S. Bassett, *The League of Nations,* chapter 14; C. Howard-Ellis, *The Origin, Structure and Working of the League of Nations,* pp. 141-153; *Minutes of the Committee on the Composition of the Council* (League Doc. C. 299. M. 139. 1926 V).

[14] *O. J.,* 1926, p. 498.

Germany remained firm in her declaration that she would not enter the League if any other power was to be given a permanent seat at the same time. France continued to insist either that Poland be granted a permanent seat or that she be given a non-permanent seat. Spain declared that, although she would agree not to vote against the admission of Germany, she would withdraw from the League. Brazil maintained her position without change.[15]

An attempt was made to break the deadlock through a series of informal conversations, chiefly among those powers signatories to the Locarno agreements, rather than by attempting to deal with the matter through the machinery of the League itself.[16] Sweden offered to break the deadlock, so far as the demands of France and Poland were concerned, by agreeing to vacate her Council seat if one of the pro-French states, Czechoslovakia or Belgium, would also resign, the vacancies thus created to be filled by Poland and a neutral state such as Holland. Inasmuch as both Czechoslovakia and Belgium expressed willingness to make this sacrifice for the good of the League, it was tentatively agreed that Poland was to have the non-permanent seat of Czechoslovakia and Holland that of Sweden. However, this proposed solution was not of such a nature as to satisfy the claims of Spain and Brazil. Neither was it reached in a manner suitable for soothing the injured pride of these states. Consequently, Spain persisted in her plan to resign from the League, and the delegate of Brazil, M. Mello-Franco, was instructed by his government to vote against a perma-

[15] Compare Bassett, p. 313.

[16] See the remarks of Dr. Nansen (Norway) in the Special Session of the assembly (March, 1926).

nent seat for Germany when that matter should be brought before the Council.

When the special Assembly, which had convened on March 8, 1926, reached, on March 17, the question of the admission of Germany to the League, Sir Austen Chamberlain (British Empire), *rapporteur* of the First Committee, which had unanimously recommended the admission of Germany to the League, asked that he might be permitted to defer his remarks until the Assembly had heard a communication to be presented by M. Mello-Franco (Brazil).[17] The representative of Brazil thereupon took the floor and announced that, since it was not the intention of the Council to meet Brazil's demand for a permanent seat, it was the intention of Brazil to prevent Germany from being granted such a seat upon her admission to the League. He concluded his remarks by declaring that his Government's instructions were " irrevocable and final." [18] M. Briand (France) suggested the following resolution which was unanimously adopted by the Assembly:

The Assembly regrets that the difficulties encountered have prevented the attainment of the purpose for which it was convened,

And expresses the hope that, between now and the ordinary September session of 1926, these difficulties may be surmounted so as to make it possible for Germany to enter the League of Nations on that occasion.[19]

Thus the Assembly found itself obliged to postpone the admission of Germany to the League until a scheme could be devised for obtaining unanimity in the Council for the plan to provide for Germany a permanent seat in that body.

[17] *Records of the Special Session of the Assembly* (March, 1926), Plenary, p. 25.

[18] *Ibid.*, p. 26.

[19] *Ibid.*, p. 32.

The first step toward working out the solution to the problem through a utilization of the official League machinery rather than through a dependence upon informal conversations and bargaining was taken by Viscount Ishii (Japan) when he announced in the Assembly, March 17, that as President of the Council he would submit a proposal to that body that they appoint a committee to study the composition of the Council and the number and mode of election of its members.[20] At a Council meeting held the next day such a committee was in fact created, to meet May 10, the membership to consist of representatives of all states having Council seats, and, in addition, representatives of the Argentine Republic, China, Germany, Poland and Switzerland.[21] The committee met and on June 10. submitted to the Council its report on the work of its first session.[22] In substance, the committee suggested that the non-permanent members of the Council be increased to nine and elected for three years each; that they take office immediately after election, one-third being elected each year; and that a retiring member may not be re-elected for three years except by a two-thirds vote of the Assembly, the number of such re-elected members not exceeding three at one time.[23] This plan devised by the Committee on the Composition of the Council received the immediate indorsement of the Council, Spain and Brazil abstaining,[24] and on

[20] Ibid., p. 28.
[21] O. J., 1926, p. 534. For the personnel of the Committee, see Committee on the Composition of the Council: Report on the Work of the First Session, p. 8 (League Doc. C. 299. M. 139. 1926 V).
[22] O. J., 1926, p. 880.
[23] Ibid., p. 990.
[24] Ibid., p. 882.

14

September 4, the Council recommended that the plan be approved by the Assembly.[25]

The appearance in the Council of the report of the Committee on the Composition of the Council was the signal for the announcement by the representatives of Spain and Brazil of the intention of their governments to withdraw from the League.[26] The Spanish delegate, M. Quer Boule, however, first made the important announcement that his government was at last prepared to ratify the proposed amendment to Article 4 of the Covenant by which the Assembly was to be given power to fix by a two-thirds majority the rules dealing with the election of the non-permanent Council members.[27] Spain, he declared, had refused to ratify because she wished to retain her temporary seat until she could become a permanent member of the Council. Since this could no longer be hoped for, the Spanish Government was now prepared to ratify. Inasmuch as France, the only other Council member which had refused ratification of the amendment proposed by the Assembly in 1922, had reversed her position after the deadlock of March, 1926, the path would now be clear for regulation of the election of the non-permanent members of the Council by a two-thirds majority vote of the Assembly.[28]

On September 8, the Assembly by a unanimous vote approved the recommendation of its First Committee that Germany be admitted to the League, and, on the same day, approved by a like vote the Council's pro-

[25] *Ibid.*, p. 1241.

[26] *Ibid.*, pp. 881 and 887.

[27] *Ibid.*, p. 870.

[28] France had apparently been motivated in her refusal of ratification by a desire to keep Belgium on the Council as a non-permanent member.

posals that Germany be accorded a permanent Council seat and that the number of non-permanent seats be increased to nine.[29] A two-thirds vote of the Assembly would, of course, have been sufficient for the admission of Germany and a majority vote would have sufficed for approval of the Council proposals for an increase in the number of permanent and non-permanent seats.

On September 15, the Assembly, by virtue of the powers accorded to it in the amendment to Article 4 of the Covenant, adopted rules for the election of the non-permanent members of the Council and the fixing of their term of office and conditions of reeligibility.[30] It will be remembered that, as was pointed out above, the third article of these rules was devised by the Assembly to prevent the League machinery from again being brought to a standstill, as it had been in March, 1926, by the veto or threat of veto by one or more of the non-permanent members of the Council. It provided that the Assembly might at any time by a two-thirds vote decide to proceed, in application of Article 4 of the Covenant, to a new election of all the non-permanent members of the Council. By this action the Assembly may be said to have greatly reduced the danger of the occurrence of Council deadlocks as a consequence of the existence of the unanimity rule.

On several occasions the Council has been obstructed and delayed by a member using the *liberum veto* to prevent the mere acceptance of a report from a committee or other body. Two such cases will be cited.

In 1928, the following resolution concerning the dispute between Lithuania and Poland in respect to the

[29] *Records of the Seventh Assembly,* Plenary, p. 36.
[30] *Ibid.,* p. 79.

expulsion of eleven Polish nationals from Lithuanian territory was placed before the Council:

The Council notes the information contained in the report of the representative of the Netherlands, approves the conclusions of the report and,

Considering that for the negotiations between Poland and Lithuania to have the successful results indicated in its resolution of December 10, 1927, it is important that these negotiations should, before the next session of the Council, have made appreciable progress,

Asks the representative of the Netherlands to submit a report at its next session in order that the Council may, if necessary, take up the question again.[31]

In this case, it should be noted, the Council was acting in its political capacity. It was in no sense acting as an arbitrator in the dispute but had, in effect, extended its good offices to the parties. Hence, although the resolution before the Council was in fact nothing other than a recommendation to the parties which, in the Assembly, could have been adopted by a majority vote, a unanimous vote of the Council, including the votes of the interested parties, was required. Such a vote could not, however, be obtained, for M. Voldemaras (Lithuania) took exception to some of the provisions of the resolution. He professed ignorance of the " conclusions of the report " referred to in the resolution and objected to the suggestion that " the negotiations should, before the next session of the Council, have made appreciable progress." [32] When the resolution was put to a vote M. Voldemaras (Lithuania) voted against it.[33] As a result of the defeat of this resolution Sir Austen Chamberlain (British Empire) was obliged to introduce the following resolution

[31] *O. J.*, 1928, p. 893.
[32] *Ibid.*, p. 894.
[33] *Ibid.*, p. 896.

which could, because of its procedural character, be adopted by majority vote:

> The Council decides to place the question of the relations between Poland and Lithuania on the agenda of the next session of the Council, and requests its rapporteur to present it with a report on the state of the negotiations on that date.[34]

This resolution was adopted by the Council.[35] It will be noted, however, that this resolution has only the effect of adjourning consideration of the report, while the resolution defeated by the negative vote of Lithuania contained an endorsement of the conclusions reached in the report submitted by the *rapporteur* and a recommendation to the states involved that their negotiations show " appreciable progress " before the date of the next Council session.

In May, 1931, the Council was prevented from adopting a report on the protection of minorities in Poland and from closing its examination of this subject owing to the opposition of a single state, Germany. In this case the *rapporteur,* M. Yoshizawa (Japan), proposed " that the Council now close its examination of this matter, taking note of the information supplied by the Polish Government, and expressing its conviction that the measures which the Polish Government has already taken, and will in the future take, in pursuance of the discussions which took place in the January session, make a real advance in the effort designed to give permanent and successful shape to the system which it had been intended to set up by the Minority Treaty of 1919 and the Upper Silesian Treaty of 1922." [36]

Dr. Curtius (Germany) asked, however, that consideration of the matter be adjourned until the Sep-

---

[34] *Ibid.,* p. 896.
[35] *Ibid.,* p. 897.
[36] *O. J.,* 1931, p. 1145.

tember session of the Council, alleging that he had not
had an opportunity of examining the report " as thoroughly as his responsibilities demanded." [37] M. Sokal
(Poland) opposed the adjournment and declared to
the Council that Dr. Curtius' remarks indicated that
he was " fully acquainted with the substance of the
question," and that his numerous quotations also indicated that he was " quite well acquainted with the
documentation provided by the Polish Government."[38]

M. Yoshizawa (Japan), *rapporteur*, urged the acceptance of the report so as " to settle the question as soon
as possible in order to secure general pacification in
this part of Europe [Upper Silesia] and establish normal relations between authorities and minorities." [39]
In this position the *rapporteur* was actively supported
by M. Francois-Poncet (France)[40] and M. Marinko-
vitch (Jugoslavia).[41] Dr. Curtius (Germany) remained
firm, however, in his opposition to the acceptance of
the report.

The Acting-President of the Council, Mr. Arthur
Henderson (British Empire) summed up the situation
by declaring " that it must be disappointing to these
members of the Council who had been present at the
January session, as it was disappointing to himself,
who had occupied the Chair on that occasion, that
there seemed no possibility of bringing this question
to a definite conclusion at the present time. . . . . In
view of the very definite opposition of one member it
was quite impossible for the Council to decide to accept
the report. . . . . One member having stressed his

[37] *Ibid.,* p. 1146.
[38] *Ibid.,* p. 1148.
[39] *Ibid.,* p. 1146.
[40] *Ibid.,* p. 1146.
[41] *Ibid.,* p. 1147.

opposition and maintained it, no other course was open to the Council than to adjourn the consideration of the report until September." [42]

Finally, mention must be made of the use to which the unanimity rule was put in the Sino-Japanese dispute which had been referred to the Council by China under Article 11 of the Covenant. As is well known, the resolution of October 24, calling upon Japan " to begin immediately and to proceed progressively with the withdrawal of its troops into the railway zone, so that the total withdrawal may be effected before the date fixed for the next meeting of the Council " (November 16, 1931), received thirteen affirmative votes and one negative, the state voting against the resolution being Japan.[43] Although the President, M. Briand (France), declared the resolution to have been " adopted unanimously, except for one vote " his remarks at the time he announced the vote indicated beyond question that he attached moral rather than legal force to it. He stated that he still ventured " to hope that, between now and November 16, the evacuation already begun, will be continued," and that the resolution adopted by the Council September 30, was still in force.[44] Had the resolution been considered as possessing legal force, a legal obligation would have been placed upon Japan to comply with its terms. Moreover, the resolution would also have definitely superseded that of September 30.

In spite of the several earlier cases in which the Council acting in a judicial capacity in consideration of disputes referred to it under Article 11 of the Covenant had ruled that the votes of the interested parties

[42] *Ibid.*, p. 1150.
[43] *O. J.*, 1931, p. 2358.
[44] *Ibid.*, p. 2359.

are not essential for the achievement of unanimity, these precedents were not cited.[45] No member of the Council challenged the interpretation placed upon the resolution of October 24 by the President. Apparently the members of the Council were not prepared to face the consequences which might have resulted from placing Japan in a position in which it would have been essential that she choose between acting in compliance with the terms of the resolution and violating the terms of the Covenant.

Thus we have seen that upon two occasions the League machinery has been brought virtually to a standstill through the use of the veto or threat of the veto in the Council; namely, in 1926 by Brazil, and in 1931 by Japan. On three other occasions the Council has been prevented from adopting a procedure which the great majority regarded as best calculated to settle the controversy before it. This was notably the case on the two occasions in which the Council was prevented by the negative vote of Roumania from referring the Hungarian Optants dispute to the World Court for an advisory opinion, and on the occasion of Germany's preventing a like disposition being made of the " Salamis " case. In several other instances, as noted above, the Council has been prevented from dealing promptly with reports laid before it and has been prevented from issuing recommendations based upon such reports.

Do these cases indicate that the existence of the unanimity rule has prevented the successful functioning of the Council or that it is likely to have such an effect in the future? To be sure, responsibility for the deadlock of 1926 can be traced in large part directly to the provisions of Articles 4 and 26 of the Covenant

[45] For a discussion of the cases here referred to, see above, pp. 141-150.

which require, respectively, unanimity in the Council for the increase of the number of permanent and non-permanent members, and unanimity for ratification of amendments to the Covenant.[46] This deadlock was directly responsible for the increase of the number of non-permanent Council members from six to nine, a change of doubtful value for the League.[47]

However, it must be noted that a repetition of Brazil's action of 1926 would now be highly improbable because of the Assembly's rule adopted September 15, 1926, in accordance with the power conferred upon it by the terms of the amendment to Article 4 of the Covenant, permitting the Assembly by a two-thirds vote to proceed at any time to a new election of all non-permanent members of the Council. This rule was adopted definitely as a means of preventing non-permanent Council members from using their seats for the purpose of obstruction in order to force concessions from the Council or Assembly. Two-thirds of the Assembly, in effect, possess the power to recall non-permanent members of the Council. Therefore, the unrestricted right to obstruct may no longer properly be attributed to all Council members. It is a prerogative belonging only to the five powers occupying permanent seats. Hence, the danger of the repetition of this evil has been decidedly reduced.

Unfortunately, however, non-permanent Council members still possess the absolute power to prevent

---

[46] The existence of the unanimity rule should not, of course, be held solely responsible for the deadlock. Had the methods employed by the Locarno signatories been different it might have been avoided. Also, there is reason to doubt whether the deadlock would have occurred had not some of the Great Powers attempted to strengthen themselves by supporting the claims of smaller states for Council seats.

[47] See William E. Rappard, *The Geneva Experiment*, Chapter 2.

the amending of the Covenant by withholding ratification, for Article 26 has been interpreted by the League
as requiring ratification by all states occupying Council seats at the time the amendment was proposed by
the Assembly, and by a majority of all members of the
League.[48] Therefore, the Assembly could not secure
the ratification of an amendment by " recalling " a non-
permanent member of the Council and electing a new
member that would be willing to ratify. It might, however, use the threat of " recall " as a weapon by which
to coerce a non-permanent Council member into acting
favorably upon an amendment to the Covenant which
was looked upon by a large majority as essential for
the well-being of the League.

In respect to the other conspicuous failure of League
machinery, namely, the failure of the Council to deal
effectively with the Sino-Japanese dispute, responsibility can not, in the opinion of the present writer, be
laid at the door of the unanimity rule, for, in the
earlier cases in which the Council had acted in a judicial capacity in dealing with disputes referred to it
under Article 11 of the Covenant, it had been held that
the votes of interested parties were not essential for
the achievement of unanimity. Hence, had the Council followed precedent, the negative vote of Japan
would not have been interpreted as preventing the resolution of October 24 from having legal force. The unanimity rule was not the insurmountable obstacle which
prevented the Council from fixing a date for the withdrawal of Japanese troops. Instead, the Council refrained from assigning legal force to the resolution
because it did not desire to put Japan in a position
which would have necessitated compliance with the

[48] *Records of the Second Assembly*, Plenary, p. 733.

terms of the resolution or resort by the League to the sanctions provided in the Covenant. The resolution failed, not because the rules governing the procedure of the League would not permit the Council to assign to it legal force in the face of the negative vote of Japan, but because the Council did not desire so to rule when a great power seemed to be prepared to follow a course of action contrary to that specified in the resolution. The unanimity rule in this case was merely a cloak behind which the Council found it convenient to take refuge.

Several instances have been noted in which the Council has been prevented from applying to the World Court for an advisory opinion because of the opposition of a single member. Obviously, in each of these cases the Council was prevented from applying that procedure best suited for bringing about a prompt settlement of the dispute. However, it seems very probable that in the future both Council and Assembly will rule that the decision to request an advisory opinion from the World Court is a procedural question to be decided, of course, by majority vote.

However, even should the Council decide that the requesting of an advisory opinion may properly be considered a procedural question to be decided by majority vote, and even should it in the future adhere very strictly to its early practice of excluding the votes of interested parties when the Council is acting in a judicial capacity, the unanimity rule would still permit considerable opportunity for obstruction and delay. This possibility has been illustrated by Lithuania's and Germany's vetoes in 1928 and 1931, respectively.

Under the unanimity rule as it is now interpreted, compromises must be reached, compromises which may weaken resolutions, in order that action may be taken with reasonable rapidity. Perhaps some delays would have been avoided and, no doubt, some undesirable compromises as well, if the plan of General Smuts and Woodrow Wilson providing that at least three members of the Council must oppose in order to veto a resolution had been adopted. However, comparatively little opportunity remains for a non-permanent member of the Council, through its opposition to the majority, seriously to obstruct the functioning of that body. The close and intimate contacts of Council representatives with each other and the devotion that many of them have to the League idea will ordinarily prevent a member from casting a negative vote which would tie up the League machinery, except in those cases in which strong political motives are at work. In such cases, the opposition may be overcome through resort to some device for defeating strict unanimity, or, if necessary, opposition may be broken down by resort to pressure through diplomatic channels, or, in extreme cases, to the threat of " recall " by the Assembly. On the other hand, strong opposition coming from one of the five powers occupying permanent Council seats, particularly if it be from one possessing great military strength, will ordinarily cause a resolution to be withdrawn or to be modified in such a way as to become acceptable to that power. It is submitted, however, that the realities of international life are such that this would still be the case even though no unanimity rule existed.

What of the future of the unanimity rule in the League of Nations? Will it be maintained? May further modification be expected? Or will it be discarded in favor of the majority principle? The question is one which has been frequently discussed in the League from its very first year of existence to the present.

Indeed, attacks upon the unanimity principle have not been infrequent.

It will be recalled that in the First Assembly the Colombian delegation, disturbed by " the danger that the negative vote of some delegation may prevent the realization of the lofty ideals which inspired the Articles of the Covenant," proposed that the Covenant be amended to permit decision by a two-thirds majority vote in the Assembly in all cases in which the resolution aims " at the development in practice of the provisions or principles laid down in the Covenant." Although the Committee on Amendments to the Covenant (London Committee) as well as the First Committee of the Second Assembly reported adversely upon the Colombian proposal, they did so because the amendment seemed unnecessary in view of the distinction which had been drawn in the Assembly between " decisions " requiring unanimity and " recommendations " requiring only a majority vote. The London Committee was of the opinion that for " decisions " " the unanimity rule, which protects the sovereignty of states, ought to be maintained." From this declaration the First Committee of the Second Assembly deduced that, since the purpose of the unanimity rule was to protect the sovereignty of states, it could not be necessary except in those cases in which the sovereignty was actually in jeopardy.

A very significant debate concerning the principle of unanimity took place in the Committee on the Composition of the Council after the importance of the matter had been duly emphasized by Brazil's action in opposing the granting of a permanent seat to Germany. Undoubtedly most of the members of the Committee believed that the unanimity rule should be maintained. They were in agreement with M. Scialoja

(Italy), who declared that "the principle of unanimity must be safeguarded at all costs" and that, should the majority principle be substituted for it, "a superstate would be created."[49] Indeed, M. Motta (Switzerland), Chairman of the Committee, was able to summarize the debate on the question by declaring "that for the purpose of the committee's discussion the unanimity rule is beyond dispute."[50]

However, the remarks of two of the representatives appear to be indicative of the existence of a desire for further modification, if not the complete abolition of the unanimity principle. M. Paul-Boncour (France) declared that in certain cases the maintenance of the rule involved such dangers that certain legal correctives should be introduced. He suggested that unanimity should never be required for determining the aggressor, for, pushed to such an absurd length, the rule would give a state a right to deny evidence.[51] M. de Brouckere (Belgium) stated that although he was not an admirer of the unanimity rule he was willing to acquiesce in its retention.[52]

The principle of unanimity was again debated in 1928, this time in the meetings of the Committee on Arbitration and Security. The debate was precipitated by the submission of a proposal prepared by the German delegation, the proposal having for its purpose the filling of the gap in the Covenant left by the deficiencies of Articles 13 and 15—a gap which would permit resort to war in case the Council failed to achieve unanimity. Clause 4 of the proposal suggested

[49] *Committee on the Composition of the Council*, Report of the Work of the First Session, p. 12 (League Doc. C. 299 M. 139. 1926 V).
[50] *Ibid.*, p. 32.
[51] *Ibid.*, p. 15.
[52] *Ibid.*, p. 20.

that it might be agreed that the Council, when acting in the capacity of arbitrator, take decisions by a simple or qualified majority, exclusive, of course, of the votes of the parties to the dispute.[53] All hope of the adoption of such a plan was destroyed, however, by the opposition of Lord Cushendun (British Empire) who made the following statement:

> The unanimity of the Council was very deliberately adopted by the framers of the Covenant. It is regarded by many states, possibly by all, as itself a very great security under many conceivable circumstances, and I think, that every time we or any other organ of the League undertake to invade that principle or to diminish that principle of unanimity on the Council, although it may serve the particular purpose we have in view at the moment, it will in the long run both weaken the League of Nations itself and undermine the confidence which many states, and probably all of us, feel in it at the present time.[54]

In 1929, the question was again discussed, this time in the Third Committee of the Tenth Assembly, in connection with its consideration of the Draft Convention for Financial Assistance in Case of War or Threat of War. Article 26 of this draft convention provided that the decision to make a loan to states victims of aggression shall be taken by the Council by unanimous vote of all members present at the meeting, the votes of the representatives of the parties to the dispute not being included in determining unanimity.[55] To this provision for unanimity exclusive of the parties, several members of the Third Committee took exception. Sir George Foster (Canada) reminded the Committee that, at important meetings of the Assembly and the

53 *Minutes of the Second Session of the Committee on Arbitration and Security*, p. 225 (League Doc. C. 165 M. 50. 1928 IX).
54 *Ibid.*, p. 102.
55 *Records of the Tenth Assembly*, Third Committee, p. 60.

Council in March, 1926, a decision was held up by one vote. Although he had always favored unanimity, particularly during the first years of the League, Sir George Foster believed that " perhaps a stage was now being reached when it might be succeeded, in certain cases, by making decisions dependent on a substantial majority." [56]

M. Cassin (France) declared that he had been impressed with the Canadian representative's observation that the unanimity rule had very often proved a serious obstacle to the settlement of important questions. He further stated that if the French delegation had only its own desires to consult it " would have had the courage to go further and say, in Article 26, that a certain specified majority—a two-thirds majority, for example—should suffice to enable the Council to set the machinery of financial assistance in motion." However, the delegation " had not wished to overload the ship." [57]

M. Cornejo (Peru) believed the majority principle essential if the Council was actually to be able to authorize financial assistance for the victim of aggression because " the nation which was in a condition to launch an attack, which had been allowed to go its way until it was in a condition to invade a small nation, could always find a friend, one vote in its favor in the Council." [58]

The agreement as finally adopted by the Eleventh Assembly provided that the decision to make a loan to states victims of aggression should be made by unanimous vote of the Council exclusive of the parties, but

[56] *Ibid.*, p. 30.
[57] *Ibid.*, p. 33.
[58] *Ibid.*, p. 41.

that all other decisions in respect to the loan be decided by majority vote exclusive of the parties.[59]

The question of unanimity next appeared in the deliberations of the Committee for the Amendment of the Covenant of the League of Nations in order to Bring It into Harmony with the Pact of Paris. M. Cot (France) proposed the following amendment to Article 13 of the Covenant:

The Members of the League agree that they will carry out in full good faith any award or decision that may be rendered. In the event of any failure to carry out such an award or decision the Council, acting by a majority, shall determine what measures of every kind should be taken to give effect thereto. The Members of the League undertake to do nothing which could impede the carrying out of such measures.[60]

M. Cot defended his proposed amendment by declaring that the question was far more one of procedure than of substance, because the decision in the case would already have been rendered by a unanimous vote exclusive of the parties. Moreover, under the unanimity rule, if the recalcitrant country could find a single state which was favorable to it, the decision would remain unexecuted. Hence, he believed that the unanimity rule in this case, should immediately be suppressed.[61]

The proposed amendment was also given active support by M. Cornejo (Peru) who declared that, although unanimity may have been desirable at the time the League was established, in the future, the small powers, particularly those of Latin America, would see no

[59] *League* Doc. A. 70, 1930.

[60] *Minutes of the Committee for the Amendment of the Covenant to Bring It into Harmony with the Pact of Paris*, p. 42. (League Doc. C. 160. M. 69. 1930 V.)

[61] *Ibid.*, p. 45.

15

reason for its maintenance.[62] Viscount Cecil (British Empire) opposed the amendment on both theoretical and practical grounds. He declared that to set aside the unanimity rule would be to set aside " one of the great fundamental principles of international law," and also suggested the dire consequences which might result from an amendment which would permit a minority made up of the six most powerful states represented on the Council to be outvoted by a majority of eight of the less powerful nations.[63] Owing to the vigorous opposition of the representative of the British Empire, M. Cot withdrew his amendment.[64]

These debates, it is believed, reveal a tendency within the League to demand more exceptions to the general rule of unanimity. This tendency has been more prominent in recent years and has related itself almost exclusively to suggesting further departures from the rule in the Council. Indeed, there is no immediate need for such changes in the Assembly, inasmuch as the rule has been almost completely circumvented by that body. Unanimity is now required in the Assembly for only two types of resolutions; namely, those embodying draft conventions and those purporting to interpret the Covenant. Logically, the Assembly could decide to dispense with the unanimity requirement in the case of the former inasmuch as such resolutions impose no legal obligations upon the member states until ratifications are secured. If the Assembly should in actual practice find itself prevented from proposing draft conventions to the member states as a result of the negative votes of a few of the smaller powers, undoubtedly unanimity for the proposal of conventions

[62] *Ibid.*, p. 46.
[63] *Ibid.*, p. 43.
[64] *Ibid.*, p. 49.

would be dispensed with, just as it has been for the voting of " recommendations " and the proposal of amendments. In the case of resolutions interpreting the Covenant, in actual practice it makes little difference whether the resolutions receive the absolute unanimity requisite for formal adoption by the Assembly or not. The Canadian resolution interpreting Article 10, for example, did not receive a unanimous vote in the Assembly, yet the interpretation therein placed upon the article is the one accepted today, for the reason that it received the approval of a large majority of the members of the Assembly, including the representatives of all the states having permanent Council seats.

The situation in which the Council finds itself, however, is quite different. As has been noted, that body has not endeavored to circumvent the unanimity rule so completely as has the Assembly, no doubt because of the belief that the necessity of attaining unanimity would not present such a serious obstacle in a body as small as the Council. However, the increased size of the Council has suggested that unanimity may become somewhat more difficult to obtain. The experience of the Council through a period of twelve years has indicated that members with special interests to protect will on occasion use their veto power to delay and obstruct. Moreover, the formation of " alliances " and " understandings " among League members has made many doubt the effectiveness of excluding merely the votes of the parties to the dispute, for it seems quite possible that the vote of an " ally " who possesses a Council seat could still be used to prevent unanimity in that body. Finally, the experience of the Assembly and of the Council itself, when acting under provisions of the Covenant or of treaties which permit decision by something less than unanimity, has done much to relieve the fear of majority decision, for that experience has conclusively demonstrated that the smaller powers make no attempt to take decisions over the heads of a minority made up of great powers.

The complete discarding of the unanimity rule in either the Council or the Assembly seems far beyond the realm of any immediate possibility. The debates in both the Assembly and the Council indicate clearly a belief on the part of most of the members that the existence of the unanimity rule, even though not adhered to strictly, constitutes a protection for the sovereignty of states. Moreover, the great powers, especially those which do not feel that a League which can act with promptness and dispatch is essential for their security, find the maintenance of the unanimity rule convenient, although frequently acquiescing or even conniving in its circumvention. Such powers find the maintenance of the rule convenient as a method for protecting their interests, for, so long as the unanimity rule remains in the Covenant, there exists a procedure which can be invoked to defeat a resolution supported by a majority. In short, a choice between different rules of law exists for those states occupying permanent Council seats. Where necessary, they may insist upon strict adherence to the unanimity rule. In cases in which they do not regard their interests as being "vital," a procedure more suited for reaching rapid decisions can be employed. Therefore, it seems highly improbable that the great powers would consent to a complete abolition of the unanimity rule. Instead, the Council's need for a simple and efficient means for arriving at rapid decisions, its need for a means of decision which will not permit the special interests of a small and, perhaps, relatively unimportant minority to obstruct, may be responsible for the formulation of more propositions to authorize the Council to take decisions by something less than absolute unanimity, as well as a continuation of the policy of tacitly ignoring the rule when it seems expedient to do so, without the rule itself being swept away.

BIBLIOGRAPHY *

BOOKS

Baker, P. J. N., *The Geneva Protocol*. London, 1925.

Baker, R. S., *Woodrow Wilson and the World Settlement*. New York, 1922, 3 vols.

Bassett, J. S., *The League of Nations*. New York, 1928.

Brierly, J. L., *The Law of Nations*. London, 1930.

Buell, R. L., *International Relations*. New York, 1925.

Conwell-Evans, T. P., *The League Council in Action*. London, 1929.

Dickinson, E. D., *The Equality of States in International Law*. Cambridge, 1920.

Dunn, F. S., *The Practice and Procedure of International Conferences*. Baltimore, 1929.

Eagleton, Clyde, *International Government*. New York, 1932.

Hoijer, Olaf, *Le Pacte de la Société des Nations*. Paris, 1926.

House, E. M., and Seymour, C., *What Really Happened at Paris*. New York, 1921.

Howard-Ellis, C., *The Origin, Structure and Working of the League of Nations*. London, 1928.

Hudson, M. O., *Current International Cooperation*. Calcutta, 1927.

Hudson, M. O., *Progress in International Organization*. Stanford University, 1932.

Hughan, J. W., *A Study of International Government*. New York, 1923.

Kluyver, C. A., *Documents on the League of Nations*. Leiden, 1920.

Lansing, Robert, *The Peace Negotiations*. Boston, 1921.

Laski, H. J., *A Grammar of Politics*. New Haven, 1929.

Marburg, T., *Development of the League of Nations Idea*. New York, 1932, 2 vols.

Miller, D. H., *The Drafting of the Covenant*. New York, 1928, 2 vols.

Morley, Felix, *The Society of Nations*. Washington, 1932.

Morrow, D. W., *The Society of Free States*. New York, 1919.

Mower, E. C., *International Government*. New York, 1931.

---

* This bibliography is not intended to be an exhaustive bibliography on the League of Nations or on any phase of its work. The intention is rather to bring together only those materials which were found directly useful in the preparation of this study.

Munch, P., *Les Origines et L'Oeuvre de la Société des Nations.* Copenhagen, 1923, 2 vols.

Percy, Eustace, *The Responsibilities of the League.* London, 1920.

Potter, P. B., *An Introduction to the Study of International Government.* New York, 1922.

Price, Burr, *The World Talks It Over.* New York, 1927.

Rappard, W. E., *International Relations as Viewed from Geneva.* New Haven, 1925.

Rappard, W. E., *The Geneva Experiment.* London, 1931.

Ray, Jean, *Commentaire du Pacte de la Société des Nations.* Paris, 1930.

Satow, E. A., *A Guide to Diplomatic Practice.* London, 1922, 2 vols.

Sayre, F. B., *Experiments in International Administration.* New York, 1919.

Schücking, W., and Wehberg, H., *Die Satzung des Völkerbundes.* Berlin, 1931, Erster Band.

Seymour, Charles, *The Intimate Papers of Colonel House.* Boston, 1928, 4 vols.

Temperley, H. W. V., *A History of the Peace Conference of Paris.* London, 1924, 6 vols.

Williams, Bruce, *State Security and the League of Nations.* Baltimore, 1927.

Williams, J. F., *Chapters on Current International Law and the League of Nations.* New York, 1929.

Wilson, Florence, *The Origins of the League Covenant.* London, 1928.

Woolf, L. S., *International Government.* New York, 1916.

ARTICLES

Baker, P. J., "The Doctrine of the Legal Equality of States," in *British Yearbook of International Law* (1923-1924), 1.

Baty, T., "The History of Majority Rule," in *Quarterly Review,* CCXVI, 1.

Heinberg, J. G., "Theories of Majority Rule," in *American Political Science Review,* XXVI, 452.

Hicks, F. C., "The Equality of States in the Hague Conferences," in *American Journal of International Law,* II, 530.

Hill, Norman L., "Unanimous Consent in International Organization," in *American Journal of International Law,* XXII, 319.

Lauterpacht, H., "Japan and the Covenant," in the *Political Quarterly,* III, no. 2.

Rappard, William E., "The Evolution of the League of Nations," in *American Political Science Review*, XXI, 792.

Williams, J. F., "The League of Nations and Unanimity," in *American Journal of International Law*, XIX, 475.

Wright, Quincey, "The Manchurian Crisis," in *American Political Science Review*, XXVI, 45.

DOCUMENTS

Publications of the League of Nations:

The Covenant of the League of Nations.

Official Journal, Sessions 1-66.

Monthly Summary of the League of Nations.

Records of the Assembly, Sessions 1-12.

Assembly Journal.

Resolutions adopted by the Assembly.

Committee on Arbitration and Security: Minutes and Reports, 1923-1930.

Preparatory Commission for the Disarmament Conference: Minutes, Sessions 1-6.

Documents of the Preparatory Commission for the Disarmament Conference, 1931.

Report of the Committee on Amendments to the Covenant, 1921.

Minutes of the Conference of States Signatories of the Protocol of Signature of the Statute of the Permanent Court of International Justice.

Minutes of the Committee on the Composition of the Council, 1926.

Minutes of the Committee for the Amendment of the Covenant of the League of Nations in order to Bring It into Harmony with the Pact of Paris, 1930.

Publications of the Permanent Court of International Justice, Series A.

Publications of the Permanent Court of International Justice, Series B.

The Treaties of Peace, 1919-1923, 2 vols. Published by Carnegie Endowment for International Peace. New York, 1924.

League of Nations Treaty Series.

INDEX